Understanding "The Second Sex"

American University Studies

Series V
Philosophy

Vol. 8

PETER LANG
New York · Berne · Frankfurt am Main

Donald L. Hatcher

Understanding
"The Second Sex"

PETER LANG
New York · Berne · Frankfurt am Main

Library of Congress Cataloging in Publication Data

Hatcher, Donald L., 1947–
  Understanding «The Second Sex».

  (American University Studies.   Series V, Philosophy;
vol. 8)
  Bibliography: p.
  1. Beauvoir, Simone de, 1908–   . Deuxième sexe.
2. Feminism – Philosophy. 3. Women – Social Conditions.
I. Title.   II. Series: American University Studies.
Series V, Philosophy; v. 8.
HQ1208.H37 1984   305.4'2'01   84-47828
ISBN 0-8204-0142-0
ISSN 0739-6392

CIP-Kurztitelaufnahme der Deutschen Bibliothek

Hatcher, Donald L.:
Understanding "The Second Sex" / Donald L.
Hatcher. – New York; Berne; Frankfurt am Main:
Lang, 1984.
  (American University Studies: Series 5, Philosophy;
  Vol. 8)
  ISBN 0-8204-0142-0

NE: American University Studies / 05

© Peter Lang Publishing, Inc., New York 1984

Printed by Lang Druck, Inc., Liebefeld/Berne (Switzerland)

TABLE OF CONTENTS

CHAPTER FOUR - PROBLEMS WITH CONJUGAL LOVE: SOCIAL AND
            ONTOLOGICAL

INTRODUCTION

This work is to a large extent the product of a number of years of teaching The Second Sex in philosophy courses which have dealt with ethical issues surrounding feminism. Of the many works at which I have looked that deal with feminism and the plight of women, Simone de Beauvoir's The Second Sex was the most comprehensive, stimulating, and philosophically rigorous. Unfortunately, for the normal student not familiar with the history of philosophy, it was at the same time the most difficult to understand, and hence, the most difficult about which to think critically. Not only does its sheer breadth, length, and complexity make the work difficult, but de Beauvoir presupposes that the reader is familiar with a good deal of Sartre's philosophy as developed in his Being and Nothingness. She also presupposes that the reader has a fair amount of knowledge of Marx, Hegel, and Nietzsche.

It would have been nice if I could have told my students to look at some secondary literature on The Second Sex which would help them in getting a handle on the work. Unfortunately, in my research I discovered that there was no such work. There were many works on Sartre, and there were a few books on de Beauvoir, yet none of these works dealt exclusively with The Second Sex. I found that no existing work fills the philosophical void of trying to get at the underlying philosophical foundations which would aid the reader in understanding the work, to explicate de Beauvoir's position, and to critically discuss some of de Beauvoir's more controversial positions concerning feminism. I decided to begin writing a book with the intention of filling this lack of scholarship in hopes that it would be of some use to future readers of The Second Sex.

One of the purposes of the first part of the book is to lay out in as clear a fashion as possible what de Beauvoir's philosophical foundations are and secondly, show how her thinking contrasts with certain traditional ways of thinking; i.e. Aristotle's essentialism. A clear understanding of her philosophical framework is essential to understanding her analyses of why women remain oppressed today. The second chapter explicates those chapters of The Second Sex which I believe to be philosophically the most important in terms of ethical issues involved with her feminism. They include her analysis of women's childhood, adolescence, married life, motherhood, and working years. It is in these chapters that a number of problematic value claims are made which are at the heart of her feminism. One such claim is that no woman should be allowed to be a traditional housewife. Another is that marriage tends to destroy the possibility of romantic love, as commonly understood. An explication and analysis of these positions and the problems which surround them will be the subject of the final chapters of this work.

As I understand much of modern feminism, de Beauvoir's position concerning marriage and the life of a housewife clearly separates her from most liberal feminists, such as Betty Friedan.[1]

Friedan has recently told women that there is nothing wrong with their desire to be wives and have families. She argues that house-work can be a noble vocation and needs only to receive the necessary social recognition of pay.[2] De Beauvoir, on the other hand, argues that no woman should be allowed even to choose to be a housewife, that it is the role of the housewife/mother that has led to and continues the oppression of women.

Before beginning the chapter on de Beauvoir's philosophical framework, something needs to be said about her method. De Beauvoir wrote The Second Sex in the forties in France. Her terminology employs the notions of "the female child," "the young girl," and "the woman." Obviously, all of the things she says about "the woman," will not be true of all women or necessarily of any particular existing woman, especially in the 1980's. As I under-stand her, when she says "the woman feels this way or that," she means that women as a class, raised in the traditional manner during the forties tend to exhibit certain behavior characteristics. She is not making any claims about individual women but about "typical women" as she understands them. One way to understand what she says is to translate her claims into the hypothetical mode,

"For all x, if x is a typical woman, x will tend to believe or behave in a certain manner."

Her purpose in The Second Sex is to understand the causes of why women as a class have been and continue to be oppressed. It is de Beauvoir's belief that they are oppressed because they do in fact, as a class, tend to exhibit certain character traits which make them ill-equipped to compete with men for equal positions in the society. These character traits are not a function of any sort of feminine nature, but are a product of women's biological, social, and existential experiences. Her claim would then be, if a young girl is raised in this way, has these experiences, education, etc., then she will probably behave in a certain way, and this behavior is what dooms her to be a second class person. However, de Beauvoir is not a determinist. No matter how compelling the social forces are which shape feminine behavior, she believes that women can always choose to change. But such a choice requires that women become conscious of the causes for their oppression and the real alternatives to the traditional feminine life style of being a housewife/mother. One of the purposes of The Second Sex is to offer other alternatives. The work is an attempt to explain the causes which shape feminine behavior so that women, by understanding those causes, can overcome the forces which oppress them. Knowledge is indeed power. I hope that this work will help further that knowledge for future readers of The Second Sex.

One further distinction which needs to be kept in mind when reading The Second Sex is the distinction between the words "male" and "female" and "masculine" and "feminine." The words "male" and "female" are gender specific and are meant to indicate certain biological differences between the sexes. "Masculine" and "feminine" refer to behavior traits which according to de Beauvoir's account are phenomena which are socially determined and need not have any real relationship to one's gender. Hence it would be entirely possible for "females" to exhibit "masculine" behavior traits; that is, those traits which the society has typically taught the male of the species to exhibit. It is de Beauvoir's position that females should exhibit the typical "masculine virtues," simply because these are the virtues which allow any person more effectively to deal with life's problems.

FOOTNOTES

[1]Betty Friedan, <u>The Second Stage</u> (New York: Summit Books, 1981).

[2]<u>Ibid.</u>, 91-123.

CHAPTER ONE

DE BEAUVOIR'S PHILOSOPHICAL FRAMEWORK

I. Introduction

For many readers The Second Sex can be a difficult book. Part
of the difficulty no doubt lies in the sheer length of the book, not
to mention its complexity. However, part of its difficulty surely
lies in de Beauvoir's own philosophical perspective which she presupposes rather than develops in the work. Unless the reader has
some understanding of de Beauvoir's philosophical framework, is
well versed in existentialism in the Sartrean tradition, and is
familiar with the Marxist and Nietzschean ideas which underlie her
analysis, many of her arguments appear as if they were merely her
prejudices. Without some understanding it is hard to see why she
says what she says. It is the purpose of this first chapter to
introduce the basic philosophical concepts which she employs
throughout the work. I will not deal in great length in this
chapter with the employment of the notion of alienated labor, simply
because that notion will be discussed at length in the analysis
of housework as alienated labor.

The first section of this chapter will explicate de Beauvoir's
critique of the Aristotelean tradition, a tradition which has tried
to explain woman's secondary role in society wholly in biological
terms. This is an important beginning point for understanding her

analysis, because it is easier to grasp a new position if one sees how it differs from and reacts to some better known traditional alternatives.

The initial chapters of The Second Sex, which include de Beauvoir's critiques of the biological (Aristotelean), psychological (Freudian), and historical (Marxian) perspectives not only set her apart from the tradition but allow her also to introduce and employ her own basic philosophical concepts; i.e., her idea of human nature which is grounded in the Sartrean ontology, the importance of labor for self-realization, and the psychological notion of ressentiment in the Nietzschean tradition.

II. Overcoming the Aristotelean Tradition

Explanations of the plight of women, which attempt to justify their plight as second class citizens, are nothing new in the history of Western thought. It is important for a book which seeks to liberate women for an equal status in society to show why these traditional justifications were grounded upon faulty philosophical assumptions. This is surely why de Beauvoir begins The Second Sex with an attack upon the Aristotelean or biological way of understanding women. In that chapter de Beauvoir argues that even though there are obvious biological differences between men and women, these differences are not sufficient to explain the differences in the treatment of the two sexes normally found in all societies.

Her arguments attack a whole tradition of thinkers, including Aristotle, Hegel and Freud, which holds that women, because of their

nature as determined by their specific sexually related biological
characteristics, have a certain limited role to play in the society.
Conversely, this tradition holds that men, because of their superior
biological nature, have a certain superior role or function to play.
If we were to state this claim from the traditional Aristotelean
or essentialist point of view, the claim might be that a thing's
essential nature or definition, that is, "what a thing is," determines its purpose function, or to put it another way, the final
cause of a thing is determined by its formal cause. For example,
from this perspective, it is because of the specific nature of a
hunting dog that the hunting dog has a certain function in this
world and not some other. Or, to use an example from Sartre, it is
because of the specific nature of a paper knife that it has a certain
function as a tool.[1] Once a knife is created, it has no choice as to
what its function is or how it is to perform. In the same sense
neither does the dog. The dog's essence determines its function.
From this perspective, if it can be shown that women have a
specific biological nature, then their function will be determined
by that nature, and if that nature is essentially different from
man's, women will have an essentially different function.

Obviously, this way of understanding women (or anything for
that matter) does a good deal to limit their possibilities. Because
it was believed that women were biologically inferior to men, women
were thought to be naturally more suited for certain functions in
society and not suited for others. As Aristotle says in his
Historia Animalium,

> In all genera in which distinction of male and
> female is found, nature makes a similar differentiation
> in the mental characteristics of the two sexes.
> This differentiation is the most obvious in the case
> of human kind...In all cases, excepting those of the
> bear and leopard, the female is less spirited,...
> more savage, more simple and less cunning. The
> traces of these differentiated characteristics are
> more or less visible everywhere but they are
> especially visible where character is more developed,
> and most of all in man.
> The fact is, the nature of man is the most rounded
> off and complete, and consequently in man the
> qualities or capacities above referred to are found
> in their perfection: Hence woman is more compas-
> sionate than man, more easily moved to tears, at the
> same time is more jealous, more querulous, more
> apt to scold,...more prone to despondency and less
> hopeful than man, more void of shame or self respect,
> more false of speech, more deceptive... [2]

This line of thought gave Aristotle a "natural" or biological justi-

fication for arguing that in the family structure women are to be

seen not only as subject to men's rule, but as the property of men.[3]

Lacking the rational capacity to make intelligent decisions and to

control their emotions, it was believed that women should

obey men, the members of the species who had those capacities. In

the state, which Aristotle believed ought to be modeled upon the

family structure, which in turn was to be modeled upon the "natural

order," women were to have a subservient role. Thus for Aristotle,

any talk about the equality of the sexes would be an "unnatural" way

of seeing things.

Aristotle's view is not as antiquated as one might believe.

This same kind of thinking, based on apparent biological differences,

was still exemplified in the thought of Hegel as late as the

nineteenth century. This is obvious when he says, "The difference

between men and women is like that between animals and plants. Men
correspond to animals, while women correspond to plants because
their development is more placid and the principle that underlies
it is the rather vague unity of feeling."[4] Hegel too uses these
"natural" differences to justify very different roles for men and
women in a society.

> When women hold the helm of government, the state is
> at once in jeopardy, because women regulate their
> actions not by the demands of universality but by
> arbitrary inclinations and opinions. Women are
> educated -- who knows how? -- as it were by breathing
> in ideas, by living rather than acquiring knowledge.
> The status of manhood, on the other hand, is attained
> only by the stress of thought and much technical
> exertion....The difference in the physical characteris-
> tics of the two sexes has a rational basis and conse-
> quently acquires an intellectual and ethical
> significance. This significance is determined by the
> difference into which the ethical substantiality, as
> the concept, internally sunders itself in order that
> its vitality may become a concrete unity consequent
> upon this difference.
>   Thus one sex in mind is its self diremption into
> explicit personal self subsistence and the knowledge
> and volition of free universality....The other sex
> is mind maintaining itself in unity as volition of
> the substantive, but knowledge and volition of the
> substantive, in the form of concrete individuality and
> feeling. In relation to externality, the former is
> powerful and active, the latter passive and subjective.
> It follows that man has his actual substantive life
> in the state, in learning, and so forth, as well as
> in labor and struggle with the external world and
> with himself...woman on the other hand, has her
> substantive destiny in the family, and to be imbued with
> piety is her ethical frame of mind.[5]

Freudian psychology is yet another example of the kind of
thinking which is built on the belief that women have certain
inherent tendencies and capacities because of their biological
nature. Freud accepted the Aristotelean view that women were

biologically defective and that this limits their moral and intellectual development. The primary defect is that women lack a penis.
For Freud, male genital characteristics were considered normative;
hence the female is seen (and supposedly sees herself) as a
castrated male. A female's primary concern or desire is then the
desire to receive a penis. Her behaviors are then explained as
veiled attempts to deal with her "penis envy." She may become
neurotic, or she may become the "aggressive professional woman" who
through her aggressiveness is trying to make up for lacking a penis,
or she may become a "normal woman" who accepts her fate as a
secondary person. The normal woman accepts her biological status
and gives up her desires for an active life and passively awaits
penetration by the male as the source of her feminine fulfillment.
In a state of passivity, she awaits her true biological destiny:
motherhood. Having a baby, especially if the child is a male, is
supposed to make up for not having a penis.[6]

From these examples it is all too clear why it is tremendously
important for de Beauvoir to begin a book, which has as one of its
purposes the liberation of women for full human development, with
an attack upon the biological way of understanding women. If the
biological distinctions between the sexes are truly as significant
as thinkers like Aristotle, Hegel, and Freud thought, then all talk
of "liberating women in general for careers in politics" would be
an unjustified attempt to place women in a sphere for which at least
the great majority were by their very natures unsuited.[7] Aristotle's

position is that all of the nurturing that society could muster
could not overcome what nature's necessity had wrought. The notion
that all women should shape their own destinies through rational
individual acts of will and commitment would be sheer fantasy if
most women were by nature deficient in their rational capacity.
As Aristotle loved to point out, it is impossible to create an
actuality which was not first present by nature as a potentiality.
From this perspective, if women were for the most part thought to
lack the rational capacity, then attempts at a rational education
for all women would be a supreme waste of time. In the same sense,
if most women were by nature more emotional than men, then to try
to eliminate this emotional nature through education would be as
futile as trying to teach a stone to fly by throwing it in the air
over and over and over. Hence if it could be shown that women were
by nature subject to control by their emotions and lack the rational
abilities of men, their treatment as second-class citizens would be
only the natural thing to do.

The importance of the issue for the women's movement is obvious.
But the fact that such a position would be harmful to women's
liberation by barring women from public life and the necessary
education is not sufficient grounds to give up the position. What
must be done is to supply a series of arguments which show that the
biological approach to determining women's capacities is unfounded.

De Beauvoir's methods of refuting the arguments based on
biological data are multifarious. Some attack the methods and conclusions of the scientist who looks to nature to justify his

prejudices. Others attack this whole approach of using biological data to explain human reality. First she points out that in nature as a whole for every example of male "supremacy" there is also an example of female supremacy. This is especially true in the insect and bird world.[8] Secondly, she also points out that the "objective scientist" cannot logically introduce such value terms as "supremacy" into this "value free" discipline. Because the development of any member of the animal world is profoundly influenced by its environment, the notion of "supremacy" is relative to the environment in which the member of the species finds itself.[9] For example, the strength of the brightly colored male bird may not be nearly so valuable in the struggle for existence as the camouflage of the female. "Supremacy" is relative to the environment. Hence as the environment changes, so will those traits which aid in survival.

What de Beauvoir wants to establish is that even if the males of a species are physically different from females it does not follow that these differences are nearly as significant as most traditional thinkers have supposed. Even if the male in the animal kingdom may be "larger than the female, stronger, swifter, more adventurous; he leads a more independent life, his activities are more spontaneous,"[10] these traits may not be particularly relevant in the human world.

De Beauvoir's main argument is that there is a basic difference between the animal and the human world. In the animal world the species develops certain characteristics in relation to an environment which is relatively fixed and thus the species remains fixed.

But, in the human world, de Beauvoir maintains that the environment in which humans find themselves is always changing, and thus so are humans. The environment changes through the conscious work of humans upon the environment. If at any time women appear to have certain qualities like emotionality and irrationality, de Beauvoir holds that it is because women's experiences in the world have taught them to choose and to behave in that fashion, not because of some a priori disposition genetically given. As the total lived environment changes, so too will these qualities. Her position is very clear when she says:

> It has been frequently maintained that in physiology
> alone must be sought the answers to these questions:
> Are the chances for individual success the same in
> the two sexes? Which plays the more important role
> in the species? But it must be noted that the first
> of these problems is quite different in the case of
> woman, as compared with other females; for animal
> species are fixed and it is possible to define them
> in static terms; by merely collecting observations
> it can be decided whether the mare is as fast as
> the stallion or whether male chimpanzees excel
> their mates in intelligence tests -- whereas the
> human species is forever in a state of change,
> forever becoming.[11]

In her position that the becoming of human beings is a product of labor and the corresponding change of the environment, de Beauvoir's position is reminiscent of Marx's in his Economic and Philosophical Manuscripts, where he points out that it is through labor that human beings both change the world and themselves and that the relation is dialectical; that is, as humans remake the world, so they remake themselves.[12] To talk of human beings as having a fixed essence which compels them toward this or that way of

being is to forget this dialectical process of change. While Marx
uses this model to explain that humans' apparently natural or innate
antagonism towards their fellow humans is in reality but a product
of alienated labor, de Beauvoir employs the notion of one becoming
what one is through labor to explain why women appear to have the
traits that they typically have. In both instances if society were
changed, so too would certain behaviors of the humans living in
that society.

For Marx, if the means of production were to change so that
humans no longer were forced to compete in the marketplace of a
class society, then the apparently natural antagonism between human
beings would likewise be altered towards benevolence and friendship.
In an analogous fashion for de Beauvoir if the traumas that women
experience with adolescence, menstruation, sexual initiation, and
marriage were eliminated so too would their apparent natures.

However there is one essential difference between de Beauvoir's
approach and Marx's. Throughout The Second Sex, de Beauvoir,
unlike Marx, believes that human nature is essentially antagonistic.
Even though humans may, through an act of the will, choose not to
act on their natural disposition to oppress others, conflict is
still the most basic element of human nature.[13] It should also be
pointed out that even apart from this difference, de Beauvoir is
still not adopting the strict Marxian notion of deterministic
historical materialism, which she believes is common to many
Marxists, to explain social change. In fact in chapter three, her
chapter on the Marxist account of feminine behavior which holds that

it is totally determined by the economic conditions of the society, she spends a good deal of time criticizing such a deterministic interpretation of Marx's writings. She is critical of such Marxists for their reductionist tendencies which tend to explain all human behavior in purely economic terms. For de Beauvoir, any attempt to explain human behavior without human freedom is inadequate. For that reason she is also critical of some biologists who would explain human behavior in merely physiological terms, or Freudians who attempt to explain it in merely sexual terms or unconscious drives. For her, each attempt leaves out the uniquely human element of human freedom and self-transcendence through freely chosen projects.[14] For de Beauvoir, any adequate explanation of women's behavior must include an examination of the biological differences between men and women, an analysis of the social conditions, including the existing means of production, and finally the existentialist understanding of human behavior. None of these three factors can be left out.

We have seen that in the chapter on biological explanations, de Beauvoir's point of departure is from a human perspective rather than beginning the analysis in terms of the animal kingdom in general. For de Beauvoir human reality always involves change and self-transcendence through labor. The effect of this perspective for explaining women's situation is clear when compared to the traditional Aristotelean perspective which denies the notion of essential change within the species. For de Beauvoir

> ...Man is defined as a being who is not fixed, who
> makes himself whatever he is. As Merleau-Ponty very
> justly put it, man is not a natural species; he
> is a historical idea. Woman is not a completed
> reality but rather a becoming, and it is in her
> becoming that she should be compared to man: that
> is to say her possibilities should be defined.
> What gives rise to much of the debate is the
> tendency to reduce her to what she has been, to
> what she is today, in raising the question of her
> capabilities; for the fact is the capabilities are
> clearly manifested only when they have been
> realized--but the fact is also that when we have
> to do with a being whose nature is transcendent
> action, we can never close the books.[15]

Her point is that there has been and continues to be a certain
kind of logic which says that because a certain class of people has
failed to manifest certain capacities, that class must (at least
for the most part) by nature lack those capacities. But what this
argument fails to consider is that one can never know if the class
of people has the capacity until they manifest it, and they will
never manifest the capacity until they are given the chance. And
they will not be given the chance until the society is changed from
what it has been in the past. The same kind of argument was used
by Southern whites to justify denying voting rights to blacks. They
argued that blacks lacked the intellectual capacities to be
responsible voters and so should not be allowed to vote. Ironically,
the blacks would always appear to lack those capacities until they
were given the opportunity to manifest them, and this would only
occur once they were given the right to vote. As Aristotle wrote,
"one becomes a builder only by building," and so from the oppressed
class's point of view, one develops a rational capacity only by being
allowed or forced to exercise one's rational capacities.

It is ironic that both Aristotle and Hegel had an enlightened sense for the development of human potential while at the same time they were so willing to close the book on certain classes of people as far as their potentials were concerned. The source of Aristotle's problem can be traced to his inclination to understand all things in a strict genus/species relation which includes the idea of fixed species, with essential natures which are unchanging. If man's essence is rationality, and women for the most part appear to lack that capacity, then for them to actually develop a rational capacity would be an essential change in nature. Such changes are foreign to his idea of natural development always being governed by the essential nature of the species. De Beauvoir's claim that "man is the being that is not fixed" would be alien to his way of understanding a species and nature as a whole.

De Beauvoir's existential approach is clearly grounded in a post-Darwinian tradition which emphasizes the evolutionary nature of all species. From the evolutionary perspective, human beings were indeed a part of nature and the evolutionary process. But just because humans appear to be nature's quintessential product is no reason to believe that the evolutionary process should stop. Thinkers in this tradition suggest that something beyond humans as we know them today is possible if the social forces which impede evolutionary progress can be destroyed. If the dogmas and complacencies which oppress individuals who are somewhat different from "the ordinary person" could be destroyed, then there would at least be the chance for the evolutionary process to continue to some higher development.

From de Beauvoir's perspective, if the dogmas which define woman in
an all-too-narrow mold could be overcome, surely woman would develop
to be something more than a second-class person. A good deal of
the polemics in The Second Sex can be understood as de Beauvoir's
attempt to awaken women from their "dogmatic slumbers" and narrow
visions in the hopes that they might break the imposing chains of
a tradition which prevents the full development of their capacities.

Just as Friedrich Nietzsche describes himself (Zarathustra)
as the "laughing lion with the flock of doves,"[16] de Beauvoir might
have seen herself as a laughing lion surrounded by caged doves:
women who thought that marriage, motherhood, and housework were the
natural state of affairs, or the natural order. If this is the
case, one might suspect that one of the reasons The Second Sex is
sometimes not philosophically more rigorous is because de Beauvoir
wanted to be sure that she did not find herself in Zarathustra's
position when he continually complains that "...they do not understand me, I am not a mouth for these ears."[17] If she is to be a
spokesperson who opens up new possibilities for women, who breaks
the chains of a tradition which enslaves women, she must speak in a
manner that women not trained in philosophy can understand and with
a polemical force which moves them to action. The price she pays
for this approach is a lack of rigor and careful development of many
of her arguments. However, that is not to say that one cannot con-
struct arguments out of implied premises to support her positions.

But, if one adopts an evolutionary view of human development,
as opposed to an Aristotlean view, one might imagine the following

objection to sexual equality. First, even if human beings do not
have a determinate or fixed nature, humans are still always in a
situation which limits their capacities. Human potentials are not
infinite. Basically, our human potentials are supremely limited by
one important factor: the human body. And for the most part, the
body of the female is weaker in physical strength than that of the
male. Besides the lack of strength, women, due to menstruation
and childbirth, are more restricted in physical activities than men.
Thus the female's way of dealing with the world must naturally be
more restricted than the male's, putting her at a decided disadvan-
tage. Woman, as a class, is weaker than man. If so, how can what
is weaker be equal? Why should what is weaker be treated as equal?

De Beauvoir deals with such objections by continually appealing
to her notion that values are relative to the needs of a given
situation. She points out that "whenever the physiological fact
(for instance, muscular inferiority) takes on meaning, this meaning
is at once seen as dependent on a whole context; the weakness is
revealed as such only in light of the ends which humans propose, the
instruments which are available and the laws which are established."[18]
The point here is that in a world of technology and mechanized
production, physical strength is not important. From de Beauvoir's
perspective, values are established only through a human being's
projects and their having to deal with the world. As the human
social setting and projects change, so too will what humans consider
valuable.

> It is not merely as a body, but as a body subject to
> taboos, to law, that the subject is conscious of
> himself and attains fulfillment -- it is with reference
> to certain values that he evaluates himself. And,
> once again, it is not upon physiology that values
> can be based; rather, the facts of biology take on
> the values that the existent bestows upon them. If
> the respect or the fear inspired by woman prevents
> the use of violence towards her, then the muscular
> superiority of the males is no source of power.[19]

Before concluding this section we should note that de Beauvoir's
view concerning the origin of human values will create a number of
problems when she tries to justify her own value system. How, if
values are whatever the existence bestows, can any value be higher
than another?

In summary, thus far we have seen the manner in which de
Beauvoir has dealt with arguments that woman's biological essence or
qualities justifies certain limitations in her capacities relative
to those of men; i.e., that she is biologically inferior to man and
thus lacks certain "valuable" capacities which man has. First, de
Beauvoir pointed out that in nature as a whole there is no necessary
connection between the sex of an animal and its strength, courage,
propensity towards active, as opposed to passive existence or
propensity towards nurturing the offspring. Nature is ambiguous
in its makeup. On the whole, there is a tendency towards male
domination, but there is nothing conclusive enough to justify the
biologically based argument that man is justified in oppressing
women due to his physiological superiority. Second, she has argued
that human reality cannot be understood in merely biological terms
because humans are the animals that through their freely chosen

projects transcend the present and change not only their environment but themselves. This point will be extremely important in our attempt to get clear on her view of authentic human behavior as always involving transcendence. Human reality is not mere repetition and immanence. Finally, she has argued that any physiological differences between men and women such as physical strength, take on significance and meaning only in relation to specific human projects in a given situation; that is to say, such qualities as physical strength have no a priori significance. She concludes that, "...body is not enough to define her as woman; there is no true living reality except as manifested by the conscious individual through activities and in the bosom of society."[20]

Such a position is radically different from the traditional view of man put forward by Aristotle which was grounded upon the notion of essence which is a priori. De Beauvoir's existentialist approach is clearly an echo of Sartre's dictum, "...existence comes before essence."[21] Human existence as lived determines one's essence, rather than some fixed human essence determining human existence. Human existence is to be understood as a dynamic interplay among human freedom, biological forces, and social structures.

III. De Beauvoir's Ontology

De Beauvoir's arguments against the biological interpretation of human beings have shown that she believes human reality to be qualitatively different from that of animals. Humans are not a fixed species in the Aristotelean sense, but are always transcending

the present towards an envisioned future. This transcendence is
manifested through human labor.

Before a theory which explains and criticizes the situation in
which most women find themselves can be formed, a clear view of
the ontology which provides the framework for the explanation and
criticism needs to be set forth. De Beauvoir's ontology not only
provides us with a way of understanding her criticisms of the life
most women lead, but what is more important is that it allows us to
see what sort of an ideal life de Beauvoir will put forth as the goal.
In other words, one's ontology or what it is to be a human being at
the most fundamental level, will determine the possibilities open
for human beings. To use an example from ethics, if human beings are
not ontologically free, if they are not ontologically different from
other things in our phenomenal world, then any ideal of human action
which emphasizes doing one's ethical duty is senseless. The goal
of moral excellence for humans requires an ontology which includes
human freedom. In other words, the very possibility of an ethical
life as the ideal existence for humans presupposes an ontology which
sees human beings as free. Or, to use an example from Aristotle,
his ontology of human beings defined man as the rational animal.
The essential characteristic for human beings, that which separated
man from all other creatures, was rationality. Here rationality
becomes the essence of human beings and at the same time determines
that man is the animal who "by nature desires to know." That is to
say, man because of his essential nature, has a natural disposition
to seek knowledge and understanding. Hence, one's ontology serves

a triple function. First, ontology, through defining the being of man, defines the possible for persons. Secondly, ontology allows one to see that human beings, because of their very nature or being, have certain natural tendencies or dispositions. And finally, ontology provides the goal or final cause for human existence. In Aristotle's case, this final cause is to manifest one's rationality at the highest level, i.e., contemplation.

Hence, in so far as ontology defines what is possible for humans, it provides in itself a sort of ethical standard. For example, if one's ontology holds that human beings are the kinds of beings who are not fixed but must always transcend themselves and are always in a state of becoming, for a person to try to deny this essential characteristic and live as a thing or an animal is for that person to be an "inauthentic" human being. That is, the person has chosen to live at a less than human level. The person has chosen behavior which is inappropriate for humans. To choose to do so or to be forced to do so is immoral for de Beauvoir.

Secondly, because ontology defines human beings in such a way that certain natural tendencies or dispositions follow from the definition, ontology provides the foundation for one's understanding of "human nature" in the everyday sense of the term. The Second Sex does not use the word "ontology," but does go on and on talking about certain natural tendencies or dispositions. From what de Beauvoir says about these natural tendencies and her admission in the Force of Circumstances that she presupposes Sartre's ontology, it is possible to get very clear on just what she considers the nature of human beings to be at its most fundamental level.[22] To repeat, this is important because what it is to be truly a human determines both a standard for criticizing inauthentic behavior, a way of projecting what sorts of activities are possible for humans, and a way of understanding human tendencies and dispositions.

Let us first look at what de Beauvoir says in The Second Sex about human nature or the natural inclinations present in all humans. Then we can move to the Sartrean ontology of Being and Nothingness upon which her view of human nature is grounded. Once we are reasonably clear on de Beauvoir's ontology, then we can see why her ontology leads her to emphasize the importance of meaningful, self-transcending labor for human beings. One final link in her conceptual framework will then be added, that is the psychological notion of ressentiment or sublimation which is taken from Nietzschean and Freudian frameworks. This is an important notion for de Beauvoir's analysis of feminine behavior simply because she employs it to explain why women, once they are denied a meaningful outlet for their natural human desires, act the way they typically do. While her ontology defines what is natural in terms of human desires and dispositions, her use of the psychological concept of ressentiment allows her to explain certain human behaviors which are the result of the frustration of natural impulses or from guilt over acting in accordance with those impulses when such action contradicts the person's self-concept.

A. De Beauvoir's View of Human Nature

De Beauvoir's view of human nature is no mystery. From the beginning of The Second Sex she continually talks about the natural disposition of all humans to set themselves up as essential or as sovereign subjects and to attempt to turn all others into inessential beings or the other.[23] To turn other persons into the other is to subjugate them or to place them beneath ourselves in value, to turn them into objects rather than recognizing them as free subjects.

This tendency, de Beauvoir says, "...is a fundamental category of human thought."[24] She goes on to say, that human society is not fundamentally based on Mitsein or fellowship or solidarity or friendship, but rather on hostility between humans or groups of humans.[25] The influence of Hegel, Sartre, and Freud is obvious here.[26] She says that her view of human nature follows Hegel's in so far as

> ...we find in consciousness itself a fundamental
> hostility toward every other consciousness; the
> subject can be posed only in being opposed. He
> sets himself up as the essential, as opposed to
> the other, the inessential, the object....No
> subject will readily volunteer to become the object,
> the inessential,...The Other is posed as such by
> the One in defining himself as the One.[27]

Later in her critique of Marx's assumption that man is by nature a friendly, "species being" she says,

> If the original relation between man and his fellows
> was exclusively a relation of friendship, we could
> not account for any type of enslavement; but no,
> this phenomenon is a result of the imperialism of

> human consciousness, seeking always to exercise its
> sovereignty in objective fashion. If the human
> consciousness had not included the original cate-
> gory of the other, the invention of the bronze
> tool (by itself) could not have caused the
> oppression of women.[28]

Human nature is essentially antagonistic towards others; each person is always trying to impose his or her sovereignty upon the other. There is no natural reciprocity between humans. If a reciprocal relation appears to exist, it is not because of benevolence, but because "both are able to resist this imposition."[29] Hence, reciprocal relations can only result from a situation of more or less equal power where each is able to resist the dominance of the other. In a social setting, a situation of equal power is the only way to escape the domination and oppression of the more powerful individuals. Her Hobbesian view of human's natural disposition to oppress others might in practice make any sort of congenial human relations impossible if it were not for her remarks concerning a human being's ability to choose not to act on this propensity.

> It is possible to rise above this conflict if each
> individual freely recognizes the other, each
> regarding himself and the other simultaneously as
> object and as subject in a reciprocal manner. But
> friendship and generosity, which alone permit in
> actuality this recognition of free beings, are not
> facile virtues; they are assuredly man's highest
> achievement, and through that achievement he is to
> be found in his true nature. But this true nature
> is that of a struggle unceasingly begun,
> unceasingly abolished; it requires man to outdo
> himself at every moment.[30]

Hence, although human consciousness is, according to de Beauvoir, always seeking to oppress other humans, this natural

tendency can be overcome by an act of will on the part of each
person such that each chooses not to seek to oppress the other.
Whether this is a problematic notion of human relations will be
considered in a later chapter.

B. The Sartrean Basis of De Beauvoir's View

One might ask why de Beauvoir adopts this particular view of
human nature. There are alternatives. Why doesn't she believe,
like Marx, that humans are by nature species beings and benevolent
but appear antagonistic because of the economic systems under which
they labor? Or why doesn't she believe, like the behaviorists,
that there are no innate human tendencies, that all dispositions are
developed through the interactions of individuals and the environment? Hence if the society were to be changed, so too would the
apparent human tendencies. From this perspective, in the case of
feminine oppression, if one changed the social conditions, the
tendency for men to oppress women would also change. Ironically,
in one of the volumes of her autobiography, The Force of Circumstance, she does say that if she were to rewrite The Second Sex, she
would modify her position towards such a view of human nature.

> I should take a more materialistic position...I
> should base the notion of woman as other and the
> Manichean argument it entails not on an idealistic
> and a priori struggle of consciousness, but on the
> facts of supply and demand...This modification would
> not necessitate any changes in the subsequent
> developments of my arguments. On the whole, I still
> agree with what I said. I never cherished any
> illusion of changing woman's condition; it depends
> on the future of labor in the world; it will change
> significantly only at the price of a revolution in
> production.[31]

Clearly, this later shift towards a more Marxian interpretation of women's oppression follows Sartre's shift in The Critique
of Dialectical Reason. But whatever her later modifications, in
The Second Sex de Beauvoir explains the origin of feminine
oppression in terms of an ontology adapted from Sartre's Being and
Nothingness. She does not give any argument as to why she adopts
this position; she merely says that her own ethical perspective
"is that of existential ethics."[32] Later she says, "We shall study
woman in an existential perspective...."[33] And in The Force of
Circumstance she tells us that she believed that this existential
ethics could be built on the ontology of Being and Nothingness.[34]
Hence, in order for a reader to understand and appreciate her
analysis of feminine behavior and oppression, some understanding of
Sartre's basic ontology is necessary. It underlies and justifies
much of what is written in The Second Sex. Unfortunately, Sartre's
ontology is complicated and the language of Being and Nothingness
does nothing to simplify matters. The basic ideas which need to
be explained are (1) his distinction between things and consciousness, i.e., the in-itself/for-itself distinction, (2) the
attempt of consciousness to define itself through labor, (3) consciousness' natural tendency toward "bad faith," and (4) finally
consciousness' relation to other consciousnesses.[35]

1.) Things and Consciousness:

Even though our primary concern with Sartre's ontology is to
understand his view of human consciousness, the for-itself, perhaps

the easiest access to this notion is to begin with Sartre's analysis
of what consciousness is not. The non-conscious world is composed
of things or what Sartre calls "the in-itself." This phrase means
that things are self-same or always identical with themselves.
Things are nothing more than what they are. They have a kind of
static existence. As Sartre says, "being is what it is."[36] The
being of the non-conscious world is "a fullness such that each
thing is absolutely identical with itself, and no more total
plentitude can be imagined...There is not the slightest emptiness
in being."[37] The being of the in-itself requires nothing beyond
itself. It is what it is.

Consciousness, for Sartre, is _not_ what it is. This is not as
paradoxical as it sounds. Sartre adopts the Husserlian point of
departure that "All consciousness...is consciousness _of_ something."[38]
For Sartre this means that consciousness itself has :no content."[39]
It is an emptiness or lack which, because of this lack, desires to
transcend itself and posit the objects of consciousness. These
may be objects in the world, memories, imagined objects, or in
the case of self-consciousness, the acts of consciousness themselves.
But in any case, the very being of consciousness lies in the _act_
of its relation to the objects of consciousness, while the being
of things requires no such relation. In brief, to say that
consciousness is always consciousness _of_ is to say that consciousness
has no being apart from the objects of which it is conscious. It
is a "nothingness." It has its being in another, but is not that
other.

The objects that consciousness posits do not force themselves upon consciousness. Consciousness must choose which objects or states of affairs to posit. For Sartre, this act of positing is completely free. Nothing can determine that consciousness chooses one state of affairs over another.[40] The intentional nature of consciousness is grounded wholly in consciousness. The in-itself influences the for-itself only as the for-itself wills to be influenced. Consciousness is thus wholly free. Granted, the world may present only a limited number of possible objects or options for consciousness to posit, but there is nothing in the world itself which entails that consciousness must posit or choose this or that possible object of consciousness. Consciousness, for Sartre, is completely free. In fact, he says consciousness _is_ freedom.

To say that consciousness is free is, for one thing, to say that consciousness is a _lack_ or an _emptiness_. If it had being in the sense that things have being, it would be limited by the qualities proper to the thing in the way a table is limited by its qualities. But, for Sartre, the freedom of consciousness demands that it be "no thing." However, because it _is_ only through the objects it posits, it is in some sense, whatever it posits, but is never identical with those objects or its acts. Hence Sartre can say that consciousness, the _for-itself_, "is a being which is not what it is and which is what it is not."[41] To use a concrete example, Sartre would say that a human being _is_ only in so far as the person chooses certain projects or roles in the world, but that the person is never identical with any given role. We shall see how this works in our discussion of bad faith.

Because consciousness is free, it lacks the fullness of being that things have. As a lack or an emptiness it naturally strives for the completeness of the in-itself. As Sartre says, "In its coming into existence, human reality grasps itself as an incomplete being...is its own surpassing toward what it lacks; it surpasses itself toward the particular being which it would be if it were what it is."[42] That is to say that as emptiness, the for-itself desires to give itself being, to justify its own existence. But this does not mean, according to Sartre, that consciousness desires to be a mere thing; "it does not want to lose itself in the in-itself of identity."[43] That would be to lose its freedom. What consciousness desires is "the impossible union of the for-itself and the in-itself; it would be its own foundation not as nothingness but as being and would preserve within it the necessary translucency of consciousness along with the coincidence with itself of being - in - itself."[44] This for Sartre is the fundamental desire of all consciousness to be God, the desire to be the union of the for-itself and the in-itself.

For Sartre, God is "a being who is what he is - in that he is all positivity and the foundation of the world - and at the same time a being who is not what he is and who is what he is not - in that he is self-consciousness and the necessary foundation of himself."[45] Because such a union of a being that is at once free consciousness and at the same time a necessary being which is its own foundation is impossible, "Human reality is by nature an unhappy consciousness with no possibility of surpassing its unhappy state...."[46]

> The for-itself can never reach the in-itself nor apprehend itself as being this or that,...The fundamental value, which presides over this project is exactly the in-itself-for-itself; that is, the ideal of a consciousness which would be the foundation of its own being-in-itself by the pure consciousness which it would have of itself... Man fundamentally is the desire to be God.[47]

In summation, Sartre's ontology divides the world into two categories: being-in-itself (things) and being-for-itself (consciousness). Things are characterized as fullness and self-identity. Consciousness is characterized as freedom, nothingness, lack or emptiness, but as at the same time desiring the fullness of being while remaining free; i.e., to be God. The being of consciousness lies in its relational character to the objects of consciousness, but it can never be identical with its acts. That is to say, consciousness is for Sartre only as it acts, but is not identical with any of its acts. It can never take on an identity or essence in the sense that the in-itself or things have identities or essences. It is free to be anything, while at the same time it is nothing but this freedom.

2.) Consciousness in Action: Labor:

If, for Sartre, consciousness fundamentally desires to be God, that is, to take on the being of a self-sufficient, necessary entity or in-itself while also retaining its freedom, we must examine the

various ways that this desire is manifested. Sartre does not
believe that consciousness chooses to be God per se, but rather that
the desire of consciousness to achieve the fullness of being while
at the same time being free implies that consciousness desires to
be God.[48] This desire is implicit in all that consciousness does.
In this sense all particular human projects must be interpreted in
terms of consciousness' fundamental desire to be God. As Sartre
says, "The desire of being is always realized as the desire of a
mode of being. And this desire of a mode of being expresses itself
in turn as the meaning of the myriads of concrete desires which
constitute the web of conscious life."[49] Particular acts are seen
as manifestations of a person's fundamental project, and because of
this they must always fall short of the overall goal: to be God.
However, as we have seen, consciousness is only in so far as it acts.
As Sartre says, "...the for-itself is the being which is defined by
action."[50] Or as Sartre says in "Existentialism is a Humanism,"
"Man is nothing else but that which he makes himself."[51]

It would be hard to overstress the importance of this point for
both Sartre and de Beauvoir. Whatever meaning human consciousness
takes on, it does so through action or labor. Human action is
characterized as the conscious positing of an end or goal, determining the best means to that end, and acting upon that choice. Some
ends or goals are more fundamental than others. For example, one's
choice to be a philosophy professor would be more fundamental than
one's choice to buy an automobile. The former would be more fundamental for Sartre because the goal would affect most of the secondary

choices one makes in one's life. The more fundamental choices determine the kind of life one leads. Or as Sartre says, "It is therefore the positing of my ultimate ends which characterizes my being...."[52] Hence the projects that one chooses are tremendously important in terms of what a human being becomes.

However, for Sartre there is no true identity or self which underlies a person's actions. If there were, this self would limit consciousness' freedom. For both Sartre and de Beauvoir, one is simply what one does. And because "man is wholly and forever free, each person is totally responsible for the role that is chosen."[53] Human reality is "entirely abandoned to the intolerable necessity of making itself be, down to the slightest detail."[54] There are no excuses.

Thus in the case of de Beauvoir's feminism, if a woman is unhappy because she has chosen to be a housewife, she has no one to blame but herself; that is, as long as she was cognizant of other options. And once a woman makes a choice, she is a housewife in the paradoxical sense in which a human being can be anything. The actions or labor that she performs are in fact an externalization of what she is. Hence if, as de Beauvoir says, a woman does little, then she is little.

De Beauvoir frequently emphasizes the importance of human labor. In one of the early chapters of The Second Sex she describes the importance of work for primitive man as follows: "The lesson of work is not inscribed upon a passive subject: The subject shapes and masters himself in shaping and mastering the land."[55] The consciousness which is at first nothing takes on an identity through its dialectical relation to the world. It is through labor that humans come to understand who they are. As de Beauvoir says, "In this activity (labor) he put his power to the test; he set up goals and opened up roads towards them; in brief, he found-- self-realization as an existent. To maintain, he created; he burst out of the present, he opened the future...by this transcendence he creates values that deprive pure repetition of value."[56]

Labor, from this perspective, is seen as the self-conscious externalization of inner potential. It is not like animal behavior, which is merely a blind repetitive response to the environment. Human labor freely transcends the present by consciously setting up new goals and realizing those goals through conscious deliberate activity. De Beauvoir's description of labor in her section on the historical development of women's oppression again shows the importance of labor to self-development, and moreover how the exclusion of women in the past from meaningful labor can historically explain why they appear to lack certain capacities such as reason and inventiveness, and why being excluded from that activity through which such potentials are realized, women have remained second-class persons. Man's apparent superiority is not a product of nature, but a product of his experience through labor.

> Little by little man has acted upon his experience.
> Spirit prevails over life, transcendence over
> immanence, technique over magic, and reason over
> superstition...The workman,...shapes his tools after
> his own design; with his hands he forms it according
> to his project; confronting passive nature, he

> overcomes her resistance and asserts his sovereign
> will....He comes to realize his responsibility
> for what he is making; his skills or clumsiness
> will make or break it; careful, clever he develops
> his skill to a point of perfection in which he
> takes pride:...man learns his power. In relation
> to his creative arm to the fabricated object he
> experiences causation, (he learned that)...This
> world of tools could be embraced within clear
> concepts: Rational thought, logic, mathematics
> could now appear...the reign of Homo Faber is
> the reign of time manageable as space, of
> necessary consequences, of the project of action,
> of reason.[57]

She is saying that men have developed their rational and human
capacities through labor because it is their labor in the world which
calls for rational understanding of the situation and the development of problem solving abilities. Man's greatest gifts were not
handed down from the gods but were developed out of the necessity
of dealing with the world. Women, on the other hand, have
historically been denied access to working world and thus have
tended never to develop these rational capacities. Woman saw the
world as a conglomeration of mysterious processes, not the least
of which was her own body.[58] The notion that a set of universal
principles might be used to rationally explain many particular
events or solve a great variety of seemingly unrelated problems
was foreign to woman's way of thinking. As long as woman was denied
access to the male working world, it was enough to pray, cast
spells, or converse with the hidden powers of the earth, rather
than learn to deal with problems.

It is clear from what we have seen that this notion of
authentic labor as a means to human self-realization, which is

grounded on Sartre's ontology, provides de Beauvoir with a criterion by which she can criticize most traditional "feminine roles" in the society, such as being a housekeeper, mother, and sex-object. These roles stultify human development.

In conclusion, consciousness must act. Its very being is found in its action. Hence the kind of being that a person is, is determined by the kind of actions in which one engages. These actions are determined by the kind of fundamental role or project one chooses.

3.) Bad Faith:

Although consciousness realizes itself through action, action has a negative corollary; that is, consciousness has a tendency to lie to itself in so far as it believes it is identical with the actions or roles it chooses, thus taking on the properties of the in-itself. This is what Sartre calls "bad faith." We have already seen that for Sartre, consciousness desires the fullness of being, and at the most fundamental level this is the desire to be God. Bad faith is a corollary of this desire to be a being whose existence needs no justification. To be in bad faith is to desire to take on the identity of a thing or a role such that one no longer has to continually give one's life meaning. The role that one chooses is believed to be sufficient to justify one's existence. Of course this is an explicit denial of one's freedom and the responsibility that accompanies freedom. That is why Sartre calls it "bad faith."

Such behavior takes many forms. Typical modes involve an attempt to become identical with one's role, one's vocation, one's past, or one's family. For example, it is the attempt to say, "I am (nothing but) a philosophy professor." or "I am (nothing but) a housewife" and to let those roles take away one's consciousness of one's freedom, to take away or limit one's possibilities. In the example of "being a philosophy professor," Sartre would say that one tends to adopt the behavior appropriate to "being a professor" and to deny all other possibilities. Once one adopts a role in bad faith it appears not to be necessary for consciousness to make the kind of continued decisions that authentic humans make. The role determines what is possible and what is not. The role determines what is allowable to wear, who one has or doesn't have as friends, what values must be upheld, and what one does in one's leisure. The role gives the person a sense of being something concrete. "I am a philosophy professor" thus denying the truth that human reality is always "becoming" and yet never being anything. It allows one to suppress the troublesome need to make choices, because the role one has adopted in bad faith has already prescribed what is allowable and what is not. In denying one's freedom in this manner, one is lying to oneself, denying one's true nature qua freedom.

In truth, given Sartre's ontology and his characterization of the for-itself, human beings are never really anything. Because of their freedom, humans are forced to continually choose roles throughout their lives, sometimes many roles. Most human labor in the modern world can be seen as role-playing. But humans are never identical with the role or profession they have adopted. As we have seen, humans are nothing but the roles they play, but they never are only the roles they play because this would be to deny the element of freedom which is ontologically the essence of man for Sartre. Man is the being who is what he is not and not what he is.

To adopt a certain role in "bad faith" allows one to deny the temporal element of human nature. To be in bad faith is to treat one's "present" as if it were complete in itself, void of a future which will negate the present state of one's being due to one's continually having to exercise one's freedom. It is to deny the transcendent quality of human existence. When one becomes totally immersed in "bad faith" the future is seen as just another series of "presents." If humans are what they are through action and action requires an end which is consciously chosen, this end is seen as existing in some future which is different from the present. Hence, human action, for Sartre, cannot be mere repetition.

Such a description is the one de Beauvoir uses to describe the repetitiveness of animal behavior as opposed to human activity. Animal activity lacks the transcendent element of self-surpassing.[59] Where human transcendence requires a future with new possibilities, from the "animal perspective," the future is seen as just another mode of the present. As we shall see, this notion of the repetition of the present is central in her description and critique of the life of a housewife. A housewife's daily chores are the same chores she did yesterday, and so on. Her "labor" is not truly human labor. Such a situation reduces the human spirit to a state of immanence.

The role and the values involved in the role prescribe the nature of the future as being just one more instance of the present.

Sartre points out that because of the anxiety humans experience over their freedom and non-being, to adopt a role in bad faith does tend to make life easier. Because Sartre believes humans confront their freedom in a state of anguish over continually having to choose, always having to justify their existence, bad faith is a way not to continually have to consider the possibilities of future action.

Another important aspect of bad faith is that society reinforces such behavior. The members of a society like seeing other members as orderly persons whose behavior can be predicted with certainty. Sartre uses the example of a waiter to make this point.[60] The waiter is rewarded more by the patrons of the cafe the more completely he plays the role of a waiter, the more "mechanical" his behavior.[61] If the waiter shows the patron that he is only "playing" at being a waiter, the patron becomes suspicious of his apparent insecurity. Society, through such subtle ways, demands that humans limit their freedom. When persons are not actively manifesting their freedom, they appear as dependable "things," as automatons, and one need not worry about any confrontation. When a housewife blindly goes about her duties, never questioning her role or her husband's authority, she gives both herself and her husband a sense of ease and trust. Her essence as a free self-conscious being remains hidden. She may be boring, but she is dependable.

Thus bad faith is reinforced both within the individual and by others. It makes life easier for all, but at the cost of negating the truly human element: freedom and its corresponding self-fulfilling transcendent activity.

De Beauvoir uses this notion to describe and criticize the behavior of women from childhood onward. Even though all persons tend naturally towards bad faith, she holds that women, more than men, are especially prone to bad faith. In fact, she holds that bad faith is especially appealing to all oppressed classes who would rather placidly accept their oppression than revolt. The "typical negro's behavior" can be seen as bad faith, as well as "typical feminine behavior." In both cases it appears easier to behave as one is "supposed to behave" than to transcend the present situation and actively try to break through the social bonds of oppression. To accept the role of the housewife gives a woman an excuse for being oppressed and doing nothing. "What can I do, I'm only a housewife?" Of course, such behavior never eliminates oppression. The security of bad faith is gained at the expense of freedom and the awareness of one's responsibility for one's life that such freedom entails.

Besides taking a role too seriously, there are other forms of bad faith or other ways which human beings tend to deny their freedom and become determinate things. One important mode for an analysis of feminine behavior is the attempt by many women literally to become a thing; i.e., a beautiful object. Of course men, who enjoy their control of the female, readily reinforce such behavior.

Conversely, the security offered in the life of the "pretty little housewife" is easily accepted by a woman who systematically denies her freedom. De Beauvoir also notes that the use of cosmetics by most women is an attempt to stop time and affirms the thing-like character of humans as opposed to their inner freedom or subjectivity. Here too, a woman's attempt to remain beautiful is readily reinforced by the male dominated society. Another example of bad faith which is typical of housewives is their tendency to seek their identity through owning beautiful things. The identity and worth of the person is mistakenly equated with the worth of the things with which the person has surrounded him or herself. These priceless things are relatively changeless, and so the worth of the person who possesses them appears changeless. All truly human worth as self-conscious activity is absent.[62]

In spite of the appeal of the life of bad faith, the existentialist tradition out of which de Beauvoir is operating tends to believe that bad faith, although on one hand very comforting, ultimately leads to a kind of despair. In Being and Time, Heidegger describes the life of modern man in "average-everydayness" as inauthentic and "fallen to the they (Das Man)."[63] "Fallen to the they" is bad faith in the sense that we live through others, never thinking for ourselves, always engaged in "idle talk" which forbids the questioning of life's purpose. But Heidegger says that we experience anxiety or angst when in this state of fallenness. He calls this experience the "call of conscience," an anxiety literally over "nothing" which calls humans to take charge of their lives rather than have their decisions made by the "they" in society. Such a call of conscience indicates the finitude of humans and that, because all are steadily moving towards death, to waste time is to waste one's life. This means that we do know that our lives are being lived in an inauthentic manner and that we should do something about it to regain our freedom, to create meaning apart from the daily round of "average-everydayness."[64]

This notion of the "call of conscience" is also important for de Beauvoir's method and her analysis. It allows her to write in a descriptive rather than an argumentative fashion. If the reader already feels that something is amiss in his or her life (angst), then de Beauvoir's phenomenological description of the lives of the bourgeois housewife and her husband can grasp the reader in such a way that the reader finds him or herself in the description. If living in bad faith is unqualifiedly seen as the easiest and thus most appealing way to get through life, then de Beauvoir's descriptive method would have no effect. The method can work only if the person already in some intuitive sense knows that life has more to offer.

Secondly, the notion of conscience is important for de Beauvoir's analysis because she can use it to explain women's behaviors which are subtly neurotic or vengeful or even "typically feminine." That is to say, de Beauvoir sees women as really unhappy in their inauthentic existence, but unwilling to openly admit it. Rather than openly revolt, they engage in what Nietzsche called ressentiment which she interprets as a kind of negative dialectic. For women, the problems that are faced are not necessarily aufgehoben in the Hegelian sense of the positive movement of the dialectic, but are sublimated, and pseudo-solutions take the place of positive action. For example, the frustrated housewife may simply become masochistic and turn her suffering into a virtue, or she may become a devout Christian and again see suffering and perhaps frigidity as a virtue. (Nietzsche's notion of ressentiment will be discussed later.)

4.) Consciousness and the Other:

We have seen that the ontological structure of consciousness is a kind of emptiness or lack which is only in so far as it posits objects of consciousness and engages in action. An important part of Sartre's analysis is when the object of consciousness is not a mere object, but is another human being, another consciousness. The importance of the 'other' is simply this: First consciousness defines itself through its actions. It discovers its potentials through its active relation to the world. If the world is only the world of things, the self-concept that consciousness develops is that of a mere thing. For consciousness to come to know itself as truly a human consciousness, that is as free, it must relate to other free human beings. As Hegel once wrote (and de Beauvoir tells us in the introduction to The Second Sex that she is in agreement with Hegel's position),[65] "Self consciousness exists in itself and for itself, in that, and by the fact that it exists for another self consciousness; that is to say, it is only by being acknowledged or recognized."[66] That is to say that self consciousness, apart from its being as freedom, has human existence only through having as its object another human being and being recognized as being human by the other. Because consciousness, being nothing apart from its object, becomes human only when the object of consciousness is human, if we could imagine a human being who had never been recognized as a human being by another, this person would not know what it means to be human. Consciousness is, only in so far as it has an object, and is human, only in so far as the object is human.

But what does it mean to be recognized as a human being? As we have seen in de Beauvoir's distinction between human reality and animal reality, what is essentially human about human beings is their consciousness which can fully transcend the present situation through freely chosen projects. Human freedom is realized through human projects, but the value of the project is determined by the recognition given by others. To seek recognition as a human being is then to desire to be recognized as a self-conscious creative being, and not as a mere object among others in the world. Thus if I am given recognition as a mere "body" or a thing, I am not being seen as a free, self-conscious human being. Or if my value is tied solely to my body, my worth is not truly human worth. My value becomes that of a thing. This is an obvious problem for a woman who is often recognized merely as a beautiful sex object.

From Hegel's perspective, the recognition of being human (a free self-conscious being) can only be given from another free self-conscious being; that is, recognition must be freely given by

one's peer or equal. Thus the recognition cannot be forced, as this
would be to destroy the freedom of the other and the other's
equality. Both of these conditions are necessary for "human"
recognition. The tragedy for human consciousness, in Hegel's
chapter on "Lordship and Bondage" in his Phenomenology of Mind, is
that in the initial confrontation of two human beings, where each
seeks to achieve recognition, neither is willing to give it freely.
As de Beauvoir says, "each aspires to impose its sovereignty on
the other." If a real battle follows, there are two possible
outcomes. Either one kills the other, and thus the desired human
recognition is forever missing, or one renounces his freedom and
becomes a slave, and out of fear for his life gives the mere appearance of "free" recognition to the "master." In the same sense, the
slave's recognition, the slave not being the master's equal, is of
little value. In both cases, due to the inequality and coercion,
the desired free recognition from another equal human being is
lacking.

In Hegel's story there is a dialectical inversion in the
relationship between the master and slave. The master who is
initially the essential member of the relationship becomes the
inessential or the other. This happens because the slave realizes
his truly human potentials through his labor, through actively
working in the world. Through his labor he understands his power as
a person. The master, as a man of leisure, does not realize his
potentials and is in fact dependent upon the slave's labor. Hence
through the slave's labor, the initial roles of dependency-independency

are reversed. The Other, as the slave, becomes the essential subject, that is, if the slave is willing to risk his life and revolt.

In a manner similar to Hegel's master-slave dialectic, the
Other for Sartre is at once the needed salvation for consciousness,
and at the same time its nemesis. Each consciousness needs the
other. Each desires the free recognition as a consciousness from
the other. But this desired recognition is totally under the
control of the Other. Thus the Other takes away our freedom. As
subject,

> The Other looks at me and as such he holds the secret
> of my being; he knows what I am. Thus the profound
> meaning of my being is outside of me, imprisoned in
> an absence. The Other has the advantage over me.
> Therefore in so far as I am fleeing the in-itself
> which I am without founding it, I can attempt to
> deny that being which is conferred on me from outside;
> that is, I can turn back upon the Other so as to
> make an object out of him in turn since the Other's
> objectness destroys my objectness for him.[67]

Each subject becomes an object in the eyes of the other. Each is
seen as merely a body and hence becomes the in-itself for the other.
Yet each, in its being as freedom, denies that it is an object.
In such a relation, the needed recognition is always missing. Each,
as de Beauvoir says, exemplifies "a fundamental hostility toward
every other consciousness....No subject will readily volunteer to
become the object...."[68] This hostility, if there is unequal power,
leads to human relations which resemble the master-slave relation.

As an alternative to open aggression, Sartre offers the
possibility that each consciousness might seek to gain the recognition
of the other through making the other "freely" love him. As we shall

see in Chapter IV, this attempt is itself paradoxical. How can one "force" someone to "freely" love him? This paradoxical nature of love leads Sartre to analyze sexual relations as either sadistic or masochistic. One either tries to reduce the other into sub- mission through force or one consciously reduces oneself to an object so one can seduce and hence control the other.[69]

Unlike Sartre, de Beauvoir believes that each can, through an act of will, choose to "freely recognize the other," thus over- coming the problem.[70] But as we shall see in Chapter IV, there are problems with this solution.

C. Responses to Frustration

We have seen that de Beauvoir's notion of human nature includes the idea that humans have certain natural desires or tendencies and naturally seek to fulfill them. The primary mode is through labor. Through labor humans fulfill their immediate desires and in so doing define themselves, at least in so far as free creatures can be defined. When, due to outside forces, the envisioned satisfaction does not ensue, humans naturally become frustrated. Throughout The Second Sex, de Beauvoir employs various psychological notions to explain the behaviors of the "typical female" who for a myriad of reasons is frustrated in her attempts to achieve the desired satisfactions. The concepts that she employs are closely related to Nietzsche's concept of ressentiment or the Freudian notion of sublimation.

From Nietzsche's perspective, human beings all have certain
natural desires comprising a "will to power" and seek to satisfy
these desires. When circumstances are such that the desires are not
satisfied, humans tend to do two things. First they seek to create
spiritualized substitutes for their frustrated animal desires, while
at the same time changing their frustrations into virtues. In
transforming the unattainable object of desire into something
spiritual, the object has been changed into some symbolic represen-
tation; the desire then becomes satisfiable, at least symbolically.
The initial "real" object of desire is then de-valued, and the
frustration itself is said to be of great value. As Nietzsche says
in The Genealogy of Morals that, "all instincts that do not dis-
charge themselves outwardly turn inward...thus it was that man first
developed what later he called his "soul."[71] The soul is created
and given supreme value by those persons who cannot outwardly
satisfy their natural desires. What becomes important is then the
soul and not the body. The body's frustration is then said to be
a virtue because to value the desires of the body is to value that
which is of lesser importance.

Some of the clearest examples of this transformation come from
the literature of courtly love.[72] The 'noble knight' in the
tradition of courtly love at first passionately and erotically
desires to sexually possess the young maiden, but cannot. He then
transforms or spiritualizes his thwarted erotic love by writing
poems about the merit of spiritual love or love of soul, poems of
ressentiment. These poems, however, transform what was once erotic

love into spiritual or metaphysical "affairs of the heart." In so doing, the natural desires, which in fact gave rise to the poem, are now seen as something too lowly to be worthy of a true lover. Thus the frustrated knight can spiritually overcome his sexual frustration by believing what is really mere physical lust for the maiden is a higher love of spirit over which physical separation has no power. The poems usually refer to the baseness of anyone who would be so low as to simply love a body.

Nietzsche accuses Socrates of doing this same sort of thing with philosophy when Socrates tries to separate philosophic love of truth from bodily love. From Nietzsche's perspective, this is a sure sign of Socrate's inability to satisfy his bodily desires or his fear and unwillingness to accept the consequences of being a body which dwells in the realm of becoming and hence must die. Hence, Socrates invents and emphasizes the "immortal soul" and its reason, and gives the love of it the supreme value.

Such a transformation never really satisfies the desire. Natural frustration occurs due to unfulfilled natural desires. The spiritual substitute is never as satisfying as the real material object. To combat this shortcoming, the spirit of ressentiment leads the person to devalue the original desire. The psychology is like the principle of 'sour grapes' with an added proviso: not only is what cannot be attained not worth attaining, but the abstinence from attainment itself becomes a virtue. To return to our example, in the art of courtly or romantic love, the more spiritual love becomes, the more the body is looked at in disgust. Hence, the

frustrated knight and the fair maiden locked in the castle can
rationalize their lack of sexual fulfillment by turning chastity
into a supreme value. The same movement is apparent in Platonism;
the more value that is given to the soul, the less the body is
valued until finally Socrates argues in the Phaedo that he longs
for death so he can be rid of his troublesome body. From
Nietzsche's perspective, this is pure "sour grapes." Socrates was
merely either frustrated physically or feared death and thus
compensated for it by overvaluing the intellect and "the soul."

Nietzsche's most famous example of ressentiment is his treatment of Christian morality as slave morality in On The Genealogy
of Morals. The slave qua human being naturally desires power,
wealth, sensual fulfillment, and "the good life" in general. But
being a slave these fruits of life will never be his; so out of
ressentiment the slave adopts or creates a set of Christian values
which devalue all that is naturally desired and replaces the
natural, worldly values with such unnatural values as poverty,
chastity, meekness, and the otherworldly realms of Heaven and
Hell, where those who enjoy natural desires will be punished (much
to the slave's joy).[73]

De Beauvoir is quick to adopt this scheme in The Second Sex
as a way of explaining much "feminine" behavior. She uses it
to explain women's tendency to be religious and to believe
in mysteries, miracles and the occult, as opposed to seeking rational
understanding of the world. She believes that women, as human
beings, naturally desire understanding and the power that accompanies

it, but being denied access to the world of real work, their desires and capacities for understanding are frustrated. Thus women turn to religion and mystery for their source of power because these areas value feeling and intuition and devalue the true understanding of the world that men have.[74] Unfortunately, women's willingness to continue in this manner made sure that they were continually treated as the other, radically different from men, apparently lacking by nature any rational capacity.

According to Nietzsche, the problem with ressentiment is that it never solves the problem. In Freudian terms it is a form of sublimation or transference of natural desires; the unsatisfied desires become frustrations which are internalized and fester until they distort reality more and more. In the case of women, the more man understands the rational order of the world, the more woman, who as a human being also naturally desires understanding, turns to religious mysteries always holding God out as the one kingdom man's reason cannot penetrate. But, the more she denies her natural inclinations, the more frustrations she suffers.

Ressentiment can also be understood as a kind of covert revenge that those who are denied the satisfaction of their natural desires take on their oppressors or anyone who enjoys satisfaction, a way of 'getting even'. This was Nietzsche's account of the origin of the idea in his On The Genealogy of Morals. There, according to Nietzsche's account, the slaves devalued all natural values in order to make themselves better able to accept being nothing but frustrated slaves and at the same time make their

masters feel guilty for enjoying natural pleasures: a subtle manifestation of the 'spirit of revenge'. In an analogous fashion, if
women can convince men that what is really important is God or
mystical religion, this automatically makes men feel guilty, first
for having so much pride in their rational abilities and, secondly,
for belittling women for their lack of such abilities.

The pattern of ressentiment, where each failed attempt at
fulfillment leads to another attempt at a solution, resembles in
a negative fashion the dialectic of spirit in Hegel's Phenomenology
of Mind. The difference is that for Nietzsche ressentiment does not
lead the person dialectically to absolute knowledge the way Hegel's
dialectic does. Each manifestation of ressentiment simply takes the
person further and further away from what the person really desires,
while in Hegel's dialectical tale of human spirit, consciousness
seeks freedom and rational understanding of the whole. It attempts
to realize its project in various ways, but each attempt, although
more suitable than the last, ends in a kind of contradiction or
tension between what is desired and the reality of situation.
Spirit learns from each failure and uses what it has learned in
order to move on to a more satisfactory position. The difficulties
of the old position are aufgehoben in the new stage of development.

Such a dialectical pattern is also present in de Beauvoir's
description of woman's search for autonomy and understanding, but
woman, unlike Hegel's spirit, does not progress. Woman is lost
in frustration and ressentiment. Woman becomes more irrational the
less she exercises her reason. The more she becomes a sexual object,

the more she becomes aware that beauty is the key to attracting men
and can be used as a kind of power over men's reason. Each substitute is but another move away from fulfilling her truly human
desires. The more woman weeks to become an object, the more
frustrated she becomes through denying her mental capacities. The
more frustrated she becomes, the more neurotic, moody, frigid,
and bored she becomes.

However, de Beauvoir is enough of a Marxist to believe that
woman today, frustrated as she may be, is on the verge of gaining
her freedom simply because she has finally been allowed to work.
Woman, like Hegel's slave, is ready for the "dialectical inversion." What is needed is a kind of "consciousness raising" which
lets her know her true possibilities. That is de Beauvoir's job.
In spite of a history and childhood which negate woman's human
qualities, while reinforcing the "feminine" qualities of passivity,
dependence, and submissiveness, de Beauvoir believes woman can rise
up if certain ideas come to woman's consciousness.

With these important concepts in mind we are now ready to
begin the explication and analysis of the parts of The Second Sex
which are essential to understanding de Beauvoir's position on
such issues as whether women should be allowed to be housewives,
whether marriage is compatible with love, and whether or not she
has unfairly over-emphasized the value of the typical 'masculine
virtues'.

FOOTNOTES

[1] Jean Paul Sartre, "Existentialism is a Humanism," tr.
Philip Marret, in Existentialism from Dostoevsky to Sartre, ed.
Walter Kaufmann (New York: Meridian Books, 1956), p. 287;
hereafter cited as EH.

[2] Aristotle, Historia Animalium, in Women in Western Thought,
ed. Martha Lee Osborne (New York: Random House, 1979), pp. 36-37.

[3] Ibid., p. 38.

[4] G.W.F. Hegel, Philosophy of Hegel, trans. T.M. Knox (London:
Oxford Press, 1967), p. 263.

[5] Ibid., pp. 263-64, 114.

[6] For a clear account of Freudian psychology and its implica-
tions for feminism see Rosemary Ruether's New Woman/New Earth,
pp. 137-139. While I will not dwell on de Beauvoir's critique of
Freudian psychology, it is interesting that she explains "penis
envy" by simply pointing out that of course women, especially
young girls, are envious of men. However, the envy is not because
they lack a penis (many women have never seen a penis); they are
envious because they perceive that men run the world. They are
envious of the freedom and power that men have and women typically
lack.

[7] Joyce Trebilcot points out in her article, "Sex Roles: The
Argument from Nature," in Sex Equality, ed. Jane English
(Englewood Cliffs, N.J.: Prentice-Hall, 1977), pp. 121-129, that
even if one could show that there were certain biological differences, it would not follow that all women had the same difference
in the same degree and that a just society would still be obligated
to screen all women to see who did and who did not possess the
characteristic. The point according to Tribicot is that even if
Aristotle's position were true for the most part, he is still
wrong not to allow each individual woman the chance to show she is
'deficient'.

[8] Simone de Beauvoir, The Second Sex, tr. H.M. Parshley (New
York: Vintage, 1974), p. 23; hereafter cited as SS.

[9] SS 38-39.

[10] SS 27.

58

[11]_SS_ 37.

[12]Karl Marx, _Economic and Philosophical Manuscripts_, in _The Marx-Engels Reader_, ed. Robert Tucker (New York: Norton, 1967), pp. 63-63.

[13]_SS_ XX, XVII, 52, 64, 57, 800.

[14]_SS_ 66.

[15]_SS_ 38.

[16]Friedrich Nietzsche, _Thus Spoke Zarathustra_, tr. R.J. Hollingdale (New York: Penguin Books, 1969), p. 214.

[17]_Ibid._, p. 45.

[18]_SS_ 38.

[19]_SS_ 40-41.

[20]_SS_ 14.

[21]Jean-Paul Sartre, _EH_, p. 289.

[22]Simone de Beauvoir, _Force of Circumstance_, trans. Richard Howard (New York: Putnam, 1965), p. 67.

[23]_SS_ XIX.

[24]_Ibid._

[25]_Ibid._

[26]See Freud's _Civilization and its Discontents_ (Garden City, New York: Doubleday Anchor Books, 1930).

[27]_SS_ XX-XXI.

[28]_SS_ 64.

[29]_SS_ 69.

[30] *SS* 158.

[31] de Beauvoir, *Force of Circumstance*, p. 192.

[32] *SS* XXXIII.

[33] *SS* 58.

[34] de Beauvoir, *Force of Circumstance*, p. 67.

[35] Many books have been written explicating these ideas. For a more detailed account one might look at Wilfred Desan's, *The Tragic Finale*; Francis Jeanson's, *Sartre and the Problem of Morality*; Peter Caws', *Sartre*.

[36] Jean Paul Sartre, *Being and Nothingness*, tr. Hazel Barnes (New York: Washington Square, 1969), p. 74; hereafter cited as *BN*.

[37] *Ibid.*

[38] *BN* 1i.

[39] *Ibid.*

[40] *BN* 435.

[41] *BN* 79.

[42] *BN* 89.

[43] *BN* 90.

[44] *Ibid.*

[45] *Ibid.*

[46] *Ibid.*

[47] *BN* 90, 118, 566.

[48] _BN_ 90-91.

[49] _BN_ 567.

[50] _BN_ 431.

[51] Sartre, _EH_, p. 291.

[52] _BN_ 443.

[53] _BN_ 441.

[54] Ibid.

[55] _SS_ 63.

[56] _SS_ 71-72.

[57] _SS_ 84-85.

[58] _SS_ 88-89.

[59] _SS_ 37.

[60] _BN_ 59.

[61] Ibid.

[62] See Marx' analysis of money in his _Economic and Philosophical Manuscripts_, p. 81.

[63] Martin Heidegger, _Being and Time_, tr. John Macquarrie and Edward Robinson (New York: Harper and Row, 1962), p. 167.

[64] Ibid., pp. 312-348.

[65] _SS_ XX.

[66] G.W.F. Hegel, _The Phenomenology of Mind_, tr. S. B. Baillie (New York: Harper and Row, 1967), p. 229.

[67]<u>BN</u> 363.

[68]<u>SS</u> XX-XXI.

[69]<u>BN</u> 374-378.

[70]<u>SS</u> 158.

[71]Friedrich Nietzsche, <u>On The Genealogy of Morals</u>, in <u>Existentialism</u>, ed. Robert Solomon (New York: Modern Library, 1974), p. 66.

[72]See Andreas Cappellanus, <u>The Art of Courtly Love</u>, tr. John Jay Parry (New York: Ungar Publishing, 1957).

[73]Friedrich Nietzsche, <u>On the Genealogy of Morals</u>, pp. 66-67.

[74]<u>SS</u> 78-81.

CHAPTER TWO

DE BEAUVOIR'S ANALYSIS OF WOMEN'S SITUATION

I. Introduction

Book II of The Second Sex, entitled "Woman's Life Today," deals
with a series of long and at times tedious descriptions of the
childhood development of women and the plight of adult women in the
modern world. The major sections of Book II deal with childhood,
sexual initiation, marriage, motherhood, and the independent woman.
In all of these sections de Beauvoir analyzes women's plight and
behaviors by employing her basic philosophical concepts; i.e.,
Sartre's notions of human nature, authentic labor, and bad faith,
and Nietzsche's dialectic of ressentiment.

In this chapter I will summarize de Beauvoir's position in each
of these sections and attempt to clarify what her arguments are in
support of her positions, while bringing up the critical questions
for discussion in later chapters. From our perspective, some
thirty years after the publishing of The Second Sex, the most
important sections for feminism are those which deal with
de Beauvoir's position on marriage, motherhood, and woman in the
working world. These will be treated in the greatest detail.

As previously mentioned, many contemporary feminists, such as
Betty Friedan, see de Beauvoir's position on marriage, which has
not changed, and her critique of the typical 'feminine virtues' as

too radical because they do not understand the complexity of the philosophical framework which underlies her analysis. Once the framework is clearly understood, I believe that a good case can be made for de Beauvoir's position concerning the evils of the institution of marriage and her extolling the typical "masculine virtues" over the "feminine virtues." My defense of her position will be the subject of chapters three and four.

II. Childhood

De Beauvoir begins her analysis of the childhood of women by saying:

> One is not born, but rather becomes, a woman. No biological, psychological, or economic fate determines the figure that the human female presents in society; it is civilization as a whole that produces this creature....[1]

What are the forces that make the female human being into a "woman"? According to de Beauvoir, the primary forces are those present in the female child's early development. It is there that the tendencies and dispositions are developed which start the little girl on the road to becoming a "woman." The passivity, emotionality, and thing-like behaviors which, according to de Beauvoir, women tend to manifest are all begun and reinforced in the little girl's early childhood. In short, girls display different behavior patterns than boys because they are raised in a different fashion, not because of genetic differences. Since this early training is prior to the child's realization of her autonomy, to a large extent the little girl has no real choice in the matter. Her behavior is molded by outside forces, unknown to her naive mind.

She is made what she is before she realizes that as an autonomous being she can in fact choose to be otherwise.

In many ways, both male and female infants are relatively the same. Physically up to the age of twelve the little girl is as strong as her brothers and tends to show the same mental powers.[2] How is it then that she typically ends up a "woman," with all of those "feminine" traits normally ascribed to women, and he ends up a man, "autonomous, courageous, and ruler of the world?"

De Beauvoir's answer is that it is through the female child's relation to the other, primarily her parents, that she develops these traits. In a Sartrean fashion she describes the primordial state of all humans at birth as feeling forlorn, as cut loose, or thrown into the world. Bad faith is present even in the cradle. "In flight from freedom, his subjectivity would fain lose himself in the bosom of the whole...he wants to allow the solidity of the in-itself, the en-soi, to be petrified into a thing. It is especially when he is fixed by the gaze of the other persons that he appears to himself as being one."[3]

Both girls and boys naturally desire the comfort of thinghood. Both desire to remain part of the whole, rather than autonomous, decision making, responsible human beings. For both, bad faith is present from the beginning. Hence the difference in character between boys and girls must be caused by some other person's response to each child's primordial desire to remain in a state of immanence, to deny its freedom. In bad faith both seek naturally to compensate for the catastrophe by projecting their existence into an image.[4]

They take on a role. But the role that each adopts is determined
not by an autonomous choice, but by the relation of the child to
its parents.

Parents, according to de Beauvoir, typically react differently
to male children than to females. The little girl is allowed to
remain in the close physical comfort of the mother longer than the
boy. She is allowed to remain dependent and deny her freedom. She
is allowed more kisses and caresses. She is prized for her appearance, her coquetry, her play-acting. Her bad faith is in fact
reinforced. Boys, however, are not treated in the same way. "He is
told that a man does not asked to be kissed...A man doesn't look
at himself in mirrors...A man doesn't cry."[5] The male child is
forced to be free and to control his passions, to take responsibility for his fate; i.e., to be human. The approval the male child
attains is through becoming independent of adults. "He will please
them by not appearing to please them."[6] Autonomy and independence
are encouraged rather than doll-like behavior and appearance which
are predominant in the female's character.

Hence, the passivity that appears to be an essential characteristic of "the feminine" is developed and reinforced from the
female child's early years. She is never made to control herself,
but rather allowed to let her emotions go. She is never encouraged
to assert her subjective freedom. Such "feminine virtues" as
beauty, coquetry, and appearance are all passive virtues. The
weaker and more fragile she can appear, the more she is rewarded. In
effect, she is taught to behave like the little dolls with which she

plays. In fact, de Beauvoir points out, the little girl's entire being takes on the character of an inert passive object rather than a human being and all that the notion entails: freedom, creativity, rationality, transcendence, etc.[7]

As a doll, the little girl lives for others; she is affirmed over and over again for her appearance rather than for any real active or "human" ability. Her human autonomy is thus thwarted before she ever has the chance to realize her freedom. Sadly, the less she exercises her autonomy, the less she is able to exercise it. She becomes nothing because she is nothing. She is nothing because she does nothing.[8] She is made to think early on that the purpose of life for a woman is to be a sexual object, a wife, and a mother. Partly, this is because the only role-model of a woman that she has is that of just that: her own mother.[9] From de Beauvoir's perspective, the typical mother is not exactly a paradigm of human self-fulfillment. If the little girl ever desires to have the adventures of a boy she is ridiculed as a "tomboy." As she grows older her work around the house does not encourage an under-standing of the rational order of the world, but is rather the repetitious stultifying labor of housework.[10]

Given such a situation, the little girl is quick to see that it is indeed a "man's world." She sees that men control the world. All of the heroes in literature are men, not to mention the politicians, the business men, and the gods. Hence it is only natural for a girl to believe that success in such a world is achieved through attaching one's self to a man. To do this, all that

the girl needs to do is to be pretty. If she is pretty enough, she
can "catch" a man, get married, and become just like her mother.
For the most part, the little girl's history is written early in
life.

Because such a stultified existence is not a truly human life,
at least by de Beauvoir's standards, she says that there is typically
a revolt by the young girl against this fate which she so clearly
sees. The young girl soon sees that being human and being a woman
are contradictory vocations. Thus, girls typically begin to wish
they were boys. They feel that to accept their role as a woman is
to close the future.[11] The male, on the other hand, has a future
which invites self-transcendence.

Thus, from an early age a girl's natural human development is
frustrated. The exuberance that is denied to the girl soon turns
into a kind of nervousness. Lacking an outlet for her natural
desires, ressentiment begins to set in. Her frustrated desires turn
inward and are transformed into wild imaginations, day dreams of
adventures, or fidgety behavior. The natural desire has been internalized and spiritualized by Nietzsche's sense. As de Beauvoir
points out, it is the female child who typically writes poetry or
love songs, dreams of adventures, which in reality will never be
hers.[12] Lacking outward expression, the passions turn inward and
are transformed into artistic fantasies of meager merit.

As the girl grows older, there is the added trauma of feeling
oneself as a sexual object for men. Even though sexuality is her
means to what she perceives as the proper life, the experience of

being made an object is traumatic. The young girl begins to notice
the eyes of men upon her. She is continually being made an object
by their looks. At the same time she typically begins to menstruate.
Given such experiences, the girl clearly realizes that her role is
to be a sexual being for man. The meaning of her existence is to be
tied to another. "She is twelve years old and already her story is
written in the heavens."[13] Despair typically sets in. The girl
dreads her future which is already being closed off. "Human
potential" is but an empty word for the developing female.

In an earlier chapter, de Beauvoir describes the development
of primitive man's capacities through the risk of life, adventure,
and meaningful labor. In her chapter on the girl's childhood this
story is repeated. Where early man was portrayed as being forced to
develop his capacities through his relation to a hostile environment,
the male child in the modern world is encouraged to develop his
capacities (both mental and physical) through his relation to his
world as a child. He is encouraged to explore the neighborhood, to
climb trees, to learn to fix his toys, to play rough, but to control
his emotions when the roughness results in pain, to be independent
and inquisitive. From de Beauvoir's perspective the history of
man is to some degree repeated in each child.

> He undertakes, he invents, he dares. Certainly he
> tests himself also as if he were another; he
> challenges his own manhood, and many problems result
> in relation to other children and adults. But what
> is very important is that there is no fundamental
> opposition between his concern for that objective
> figure which is his and his will to self-realization
> in concrete projects. It is by doing that he creates
> his existence, both is one and the same action.[14]

The story is not the same for women.

> There is from the beginning a conflict between her
> autonomous existence and her objective self...
> She is taught to please...She must make herself an
> object; she should therefore renounce her autonomy.
> She is treated like a live doll and is refused
> liberty. Thus a vicious circle is formed; for the
> less she exercises her freedom to understand, to
> grasp, to discover the world about her, the less
> resources she will find within herself as subject.
> If she were encouraged in it she could display the
> same lively exuberance, the same curiosity, the
> same initiative, the same hardihood, as a boy.[15]

This is the heart of de Beauvoir's criticism of most "feminine"
behavior throughout a woman's life. A woman is forever a subject,
who behaves like an object. She never develops the natural virtues
that men are forced to develop at an early age. It is the failure
to develop these natural virtues that damns her to continual
oppression, frustration, ressentiment and revenge. The young girl
"knows already that to accept herself as a woman is to be resigned
to mutilate herself...Life only repeats itself in her, without
going anywhere; firmly set in her role as housekeeper, she puts a
stop to the expansion of existence, she becomes obstacle and
negation...."[16] What might free her is destroyed long before it
has a chance to bloom.

III. The Young Girl

De Beauvoir continues her description and analysis of the
plight of the female child in the chapter on "the young girl." She
begins here with the girl at puberty, at the point where the girl
spends most of her time thinking about boys. This is only natural;

since childhood she has been taught that man is master of the world and that her success depends on getting a husband, hopefully a successful husband. "There is unanimous agreement that getting a husband--or in some cases a 'protector'--is for her the most important of undertakings."[17] Man is the other through which she will define herself. He is the "essential"; she the inessential. She resigns herself to man because this appears to be the most sensible thing to do. All of her past experiences have led up to that conclusion.

If the young girl were lucky enough not to feel inferior in relation to boys up to this point in her life, certain physical occurrences now tend to convince her that she is inferior. Her breasts become a burden; the hormonal imbalances of adolescence create psychological instability; menstruation is painful. De Beauvoir points out that at a time when males are going through "a real apprenticeship in violence, when their aggressiveness is developed, their love for competition, ... it is just this time the girl gives up rough games."[18] The girl, being at this time physically limited, "...never knows the conquering pride of a boy who pins his opponent's shoulders to the ground."[19] She does not learn the aggressive, competitive spirit which is so helpful for success in the modern bourgeois world. She never learns what it means "to assert one's sovereignty over the world."[20] Her passivity is continually reinforced.

However, the adolescent male, through learning to use his fists, feels the power of self-reliance and sovereignty. In an almost Nietzschean fashion de Beauvoir tells us that "he does not let himself be transcended by others....Violence is the authentic proof of each one's loyalty to himself."[21] His willingness to do battle is the supreme proof of his self-transcending love of self. The young girl, on the other hand, lacking these opportunities, fails to develop the virtue of self-transcendence or pride in one's being. She is not disposed to remake the world after her own image. She is timid and passive, never daring to revolt. "She regards the existing state of affairs as something fixed,"[22] never to be directly challenged.

Being denied the outlet for the physical activity which her young body naturally desires, de Beauvoir says that the young girl typically becomes bored, giddy, and nervous. She is encouraged to "behave like a lady," which denies all of her physical desires, represses all spontaneity, all self-assertiveness. Such encouragement only complicates the problem, denying even more her human development. "...for the young woman, there is a contradiction between her status as a real human being and her vocation as a female."[23] This is perhaps the most succinct statement of the problem in the book. Becoming female is a process of self-alienation par excellence.

In this predicament with its internal contradiction, the young girl begins to emphasize the one thing that has some effect upon the male-dominated world: her sexuality. Her sexuality is power. But, as natural as this may seem, the society generally tries to suppress behaviors which might be too openly sexual. Thus again a

contradiction arises. She is told and understands that her power
lies in her sexual attractiveness: a purely animal and erotic
vocation. But on the other hand, she is told that to be alluring
one must be the perfect female, which is to be prim and proper, the
antithesis of a sexual being. This dichotomous situation gives
rise to all sorts of dialectical concatenations.

Forbidden the open erotic love of another, the young woman
often turns her love on herself. She becomes narcissistic. "She
gives herself caresses, she kisses her rounded shoulders,..."[24]
But even this "cult of the self" is ambiguous as the young girl is
unsure whether her love of herself as a sensual object is in fact
different from her desire to attract men. If she truly loves
herself, then it is impossible to give herself to a man as an
object. To become such an object would deny her subjectivity. If
she does give herself to a man, she is doomed forever as an object
in the man's hands or under his gaze. If she cannot escape that
idea, her narcissism leads to a kind of unhealthy self-love which
lacks all true relationships with others. This situation leads to
morbid daydreams, visions, analogous to the little girl's dreams
previously described.[25] As we have already seen, de Beauvoir's
notion of a human development is such that each consciousness needs
the consciousness of another free being to give it recognition;
mirrors and visions are not enough.

Because the young woman is unable to give herself to a man,
as that would be to lose what meager autonomy she has, she typically
seeks out female friends.[26] Other women do not threaten her;

they are not physically stronger; they understand her. It should be obvious that according to de Beauvoir, given the dilemmas of the young girl's existence, lesbian relationships appear to be a reasonable solution to the young girl's problems.

Although de Beauvoir does not discuss the alternative of lesbian relations to any great extent in this chapter, she does devote an entire chapter to such relations later in the book. It is easy to see, given the problems with male oppression and female dependence why lesbian relations are very appealing to many women. The kind of reciprocity and equality that friendships must have are certainly more easily found between women than in male-female relations. Also, de Beauvoir describes such relations as being good for women because they are forced, due to the absence of men, to develop those capacities for dealing with the world that only men usually develop.[27] But, regardless of the sensibility of a lesbian relationship, the young woman has a great deal of trouble overcoming all of the cultural training which tells her that that sort of thing is "unnatural." Thus even if the young girl is happier with female friends, she soon desires to be "normal."

In order for the young girl to truly desire a man she must overcome the idea that in giving herself to the man she is being reduced to an object, a sexual being to be conquered. Along those same lines, she must think of man as something other than merely a self-assertive sexual animal. So she, like the medieval knight, must romanticize or spiritualize her idea of love. Man becomes a "Prince Charming."[28] Part of the romanticization is to desire older men or movie stars. There is some logic in this. The further away her men are, the more ideal they can be imagined. And, at such a distance, there can be no real threat of possession. There is yet no hint that these gods might have feet of clay.

If the young girl actually begins to have an interest in a real existing man, the moment the man makes any physical move towards her, she is filled with anxiety. Her coquettish behavior, typical of many young women, is not unreasonable. A young woman knows that she can be an essential being, that is, a free autonomous self-consciousness being, only by being the seducer without ever being caught in the web of a real relation. "Proud she is of catching male interest, of arousing admiration, but what revolts her is to be caught in return."[29] To be caught would be to lose her freedom, to lose her powers, to be turned into an object, a slave.

De Beauvoir believes that this approach-avoidance behavior explains not only why young girls, but some adult women are always coquettish in their behavior. The cause is the paradox of love that continues throughout a woman's life. A woman can maintain her freedom only through arousing male desire, but once the desire moves to its "natural" conclusion, she is no longer the autonomous being that she envisions herself. She has been made an object by the man: a love object, a wife, a mother.

De Beauvoir points out that even a man's glance at the flirtatious young female makes her at once feel the power of her seductiveness, but at the same time that she has been transformed into an object for examination. What a man sees is a body, not an autonomous human being or mind. She may then do her best to show that she is but a little girl playing at love and is not serious. She may laugh, giggle, and even engage in contemptuous behaviors.

Her nature is divided against itself. She wants to have a man as that is the way she perceives her future hopes, but she does not want to lose her independence and become mere prey for the male animal. This is one of the basic contradictions of romantic love and will be discussed more fully in the following chapters. The question is, how is it possible for love to be healthy for both the man and the woman if it always ends in turning one or the other into an object? Can love but help destroy freedom?

De Beauvoir suggests at the end of the chapter that one partial solution to the problem would be if the young girl did not grow up in a society where "the mores authorize women to profit as wife or mistress from privileges held by certain men...."[30] This is a prelude to her position developed in the later parts of the book which argues that the option for a woman to be a housewife-mother should be abolished.

IV. Sexual Initiation

Most young girls do not become lesbians, nor do they remain coquettish flirts, never to be caught. Sooner or later, the young girl is caught, courted, married and seduced--not necessarily in that order. De Beauvoir's analysis of sexual initiation is important because it shows why sex in marriage is likely to be doomed to failure, which in turn is one reason de Beauvoir is against marriage.

For biological, psychological, cultural, and philosophical reasons the initial sexual experience is seldom rewarding for the young girl. Biologically the initial experience is painful. Because sex is seen as a man's marital right, the man often forces himself on the young bride with little concern for the physical pain involved. Psychologically, the girl feels herself an object in the hands of the man. She feels herself being violated, impaled. She is forced to "serve" the man, hence giving up her autonomy. Socially, having lost the prize of virginity, she experiences a certain loss of power and personal worth. Hence, it is only natural that she would feel degraded.

Given such experiences, the possibility of truly enjoying sex becomes very slim. De Beauvoir also points out that the taboos placed upon sex by many cultures, especially Christian ones, tend to make a woman feel guilty even if she does by chance learn to enjoy intercourse. One ought not to enjoy such sinful or 'animal' pleasures, and furthermore, if she does appear to enjoy it too much, many men feel she is not a "virtuous" woman. In sexual excitement, if a woman actually becomes aggressive, this reverses the traditional roles as to how things "are supposed to be."[31] The man is active; the woman is passive. Thus the man, with his traditional values, may even discourage her enjoyment. This is obviously cutting off one's nose to spite one's face.

When a woman by nature desires the pleasure of sex, but is denied that pleasure because of her own situation or her mate's, ressentiment is a natural response. She gives value to the inhibitions which prevent giving sexual pleasure a positive value and, in so doing, devalues sex with her husband, and in fact punishes him for her lack of satisfaction. One way to do this is to become deeply involved in a religious tradition which sees sex as something one does only in order to have children, hence giving her a reason for her limited sexual activities. Or she can become frigid, which is a sure way of punishing the man for her frustrations. These frustrations, de Beauvoir says, can go much deeper than mere sexual frustrations. "...in bed the woman punishes the male for all the wrongs she feels she has endured, by offering him an insulting coldness."[32]

If the man tries to manipulate the frigid woman so she enjoys sex, this only makes the woman feel even more like an object. Ironically, even if his motives are pure, for the man to try too hard to make the woman feel pleasure is seen as but another manifestation of the man's dominating the woman, thus turning her into an object. She loses control as she is made to feel more and more passionate, and hence loses her autonomy. If, on the other hand, the man just violently takes his pleasure, this too reduces the woman to an object.[33] In either case, the woman feels that she is merely being used. Her autonomy is destroyed unless she freely gives herself to the man.

Near the end of the chapter, de Beauvoir does give us a brief description of what an ideal sexual relation would be like. Whether or not such a relation is possible, given her previous description of human nature, is an important question. She says that a truly fulfilling relation

> requires that--in love, affection, sensuality--woman
> succeeds in overcoming her passivity and establishes
> a relation of reciprocity with her partner. The
> dissimilarity that exists between the eroticism of
> the male and that of the female creates insoluble
> problems as long as there is a "battle of the
> sexes;" they can be easily solved when woman
> finds in the man both desire and respect; if he
> lusts after her flesh while recognizing her freedom,
> she feels herself to be the essential, her integrity
> remains unimpaired while she makes herself object,
> she remains free in the submission to which she
> consents.[34]

In this description, the woman is still an object but she "makes

herself an object." The woman's autonomy remains intact. The man

recognizes this autonomy and respects it while he lusts after her

body.

De Beauvoir's description sounds optimistic, but its possi-

bility is questionable, especially after what she says about

marriage in Chapter XIII. Marriage, according to de Beauvoir,

destroys the equality needed for such recognition.[35]

V. Marriage and Motherhood

The culmination of de Beauvoir's analysis of sexual oppression

lies in her analysis of the institution of marriage and the vocation

of motherhood. Such a culmination is only natural given that,

according to de Beauvoir, all of a young girl's training has been

aimed at preparing her for the rather passive life of a housewife and

mother. These roles are typically seen as a woman's "natural

destiny." To be an "old maid" is the worst of woman's fears.[36] Such an emphasis on marriage is not the case for men. Men have seldom seen marriage as their "fundamental project" or life's ambition. This is clear from the fact that, according to de Beauvoir, no man if asked what he wanted to do with his life would answer, "Oh, I want to get married and raise a family."[37] A man's life project may include marriage, but the value he places on it is not equal to that which a woman places on it. Because of this difference in importance, marriage itself must be analyzed for women in radically different terms than for men.

De Beauvoir carefully examines the basic differences for men and women in order to show how the differences within the institution create inequalities that in turn make marriage an institution which oppresses women. It should be noted that ironically, from the male point of view, these inequalities, while apparently beneficial for men, tend also to oppress men and destroy the needed reciprocity for fulfilling sexual and loving relations. Hence, like Hegel's master-slave dialectic, the oppressor himself is oppressed by his own oppression.

The dialectical development of this section of de Beauvoir's book is evident. The woman begins by seeking fulfillment and recognition in the most immediate and natural of pleasures: sex. When this attempt fails, the woman then turns to housework as a way of justifying her existence. When the life of a housekeeper turns out to be a boring, stultifying life, she seeks to overcome her isolation and her lack of meaningful experience through becoming a mother. When motherhood fails to fulfill her needs, she goes beyond the home and seeks satisfaction through a social life and finally through work. The pattern moves from the level of the immediate or particular in the instance of sexual experience to the level of the universal, where the woman is involved in labor in the civil society. In this respect the pattern bears a marked resemblance to the development of Hegel's Phenomenology of Mind, where in his chapters on spirit's life in the civil society human spirit seeking to know the truth moves from the level of the immediate recognition from particular persons in the family to a more universal level of recognition within the civil society.

A. Marriage as a Means to Sexual Fulfillment

As we have seen, de Beauvoir believes that from a woman's childhood onward she is trained to be a sexual object. Early in her life, a woman realizes that her only power over men lies in her sexuality. As she grows older, there is also a natural biological desire for sexual pleasure. But the society is clear in pointing out to the young lady that sexuality is condoned only within the institution of marriage.[38] Given such a situation, it is little wonder that sexuality plays such an important part in a woman's decision to get married. A man on the other hand is in a different situation. He is expected to "sow his wild oats" or play the field. Even if a woman chose to be sexually active prior to marriage, apart from the double standard which society employs in judging promiscuous women differently from men, there is the further problem of the unwanted pregnancy. Thus, given such a social situation, a woman naturally sees marriage as a means to sexual freedom and sexual fulfillment. Unfortunately, according to de Beauvoir, these desires are seldom satisfied. She claims that if one gets married for sexual fulfillment, one is probably in for a big disappointment. Marriage, as she understands it, tends to prohibit or destroy healthy sexual relationships rather than to create or enhance them.

In order to understand de Beauvoir's criticisms of the typical sexual relationship within the institution of marriage, let us return to her description of ideal sexual relationships. Once we have this ideal well in mind, we can then see why she thinks the institution of marriage tends to make the realization of such an ideal impossible.

De Beauvoir sees sex as meaningful and fulfilling only if the act is performed out of love and desire, both spontaneous emotions. She is critical of those who believe that sex is nothing more than a physical relationship, the success of which is dependent primarily on technique.[39] She delights in poking fun at the young man who thinks he is a great lover because "he has learned by heart twenty marriage manuals."[40] The ideal sexual relationship transcends mere technique or manipulation and is described as a spontaneous giving between two free and equal beings. As we previously noted in the section on sexual initiation, de Beauvoir believes that many of the problems related to sexual fulfillment can only be solved

> ...When woman finds in the male both desire and
> respect; if he lusts after her flesh while recog-
> nizing her freedom, she feels herself essential,
> her integrity remains unimpaired while she makes
> herself object, she remains free in the
> submission to which she consents. Under such
> conditions, the lovers can enjoy a common
> pleasure, in the fashion suitable to each, the
> partners each feeling the pleasure as being his
> or her own but as having the source in the other.
> The verbs to give and to receive exchange
> meanings; joy is gratitude, pleasure is
> affection. Under a concrete and carnal form
> there is a mutual recognition of the ego and of
> the other in the keenest awareness of the other
> and of the ego.[41]

Unfortunately this ideal of reciprocal desire and respect is seldom

the case. Typically, sexual relationships can better be under-

stood as one more instance of the master-slave relationship where

the man is initially trying to subjugate or objectify the woman,

and the woman seeks to control the man through enslaving him through

his passion. Sex in this sense is like a battle where each is

trying to turn the other into a thing. To be desired is to control

the one who desires, while the ideal situation involves a kind of

free give and take between equal partners. In such a relationship,

each recognizes and values the autonomy and individuality of the

other. Each is seen as an equal. The relationship is one of

reciprocity. Each desires the other as an object of sexual

pleasure, while each recognizes the subjectivity of the other. Each

freely enters the relationship with full consent and gives to the

other with willing generosity. However, no matter how appealing

such a description of the ideal relationship might sound, one has

to ask, given de Beauvoir's earlier descriptions of human nature, is such a relationship possible? It may be the case that her ontology precludes the possibility of such an ideal relationship ever being more than a mere description of the ideal.

If we are relatively clear on de Beauvoir's notion of the ideal sexual relationship, let us look at her analysis within the typical marriage in order to see why sexual fulfillment is so difficult to achieve within that institution and why de Beauvoir believes it is an instance of the master-slave relation. As we saw, one of the prerequisites for her ideal relation was that each sees the other as an equal. If such equality exists between the members of the marriage, there can be no master-slave relationship. But if the love that is given is forced because one is more powerful than another, then the person who is loved does not freely inspire the love of the other, and so his or her worth is not established any more than the master's worth is established through the slave's forced recognition. True love in this sense is the desire to be freely desired; all coercion must be absent.

According to de Beauvoir, there is seldom equality in a marital relationship. The woman is seen as subservient to the man. In the typical marriage the man rules; the woman is ruled. She is the object; he is the subject. "...she becomes his vassal."[42] The woman is _given_ in marriage, while the man _takes_ a wife. With the taking, he acquires certain _rights_; after being given, she has certain _duties_. What was in the first instance supposedly an emotional relation, now takes on the characteristics of a legal institution, where one of the wife's primary duties is having sexual intercourse with her husband. Rather than a freely given gift, sex is "a service rendered to the man; he takes his pleasure...."[43] Under such conditions the spontaneous giving by two autonomous individuals is impossible. How can one freely give what is simply one's duty? Marriage is then the enemy of erotic experience.

As a legal institution with rights and duties, marriage and love really have very little in common.[44] Marriage is a contract that the woman enters into because she believes that only then can she achieve social recognition, justify her existence as a person, and find sexual freedom. Love, on the other hand, is a spontaneous happening guided by the heart and the emotions. One "magically" falls in love; one does not decide to fall in love.[45] One simply is erotically aroused; one does not decide to become aroused. To try to turn something spontaneous into a duty is to destroy its very essence.

But this is what happens on the typical wedding night ritual, "...it is absurd to make a duty of such a delicate and difficult matter as the first intercourse. The woman is all the more frightened because the strange operation she must undergo is sacred, because society, religion, family, and friends have solemly handed her over to her husband as if to a master...."[46] And because the wedding night ritual is a duty for the man, he too may feel anxiety over his performance. The man, in doing his "duty," all too often selfishly takes his pleasure at the price of the woman's suffering. "The wedding night transforms the erotic act into a test that both parties fear their inability to meet, each being too worried by his or her own problems to be able to think generously of the other."[47]

If the contractual nature of the institution of marriage or the initial sexual encounters do not create enough frustration and resentment for the woman, de Beauvoir believes that time and familiarity will themselves assure the married couple of marginal sexual pleasure. She says that "it is pure absurdity to maintain that two married persons, bound by ties of practical, social and moral interest, will provide each other with sexual satisfaction as long as they live."[48] Erotic love is desire for an other who is desired as other. It has a magical quality which is destroyed if it becomes commonplace. Once the other becomes familiar, the otherness tends to fade away. There is no giving or conquering, there is no spontaneity. Erotic excitement then fades into the mere satisfaction of a biological need. When the erotic element of love dies, sexual relations tend to turn into "...a kind of joint masturbation."[49]

De Beauvoir does not go on and argue for a kind of "open marriage" where each spouse is allowed the freedom to choose other sexual partners. This is because her notion of sexual love is such that it would be unlikely that either member of the marriage could share the other sexually with another person. In the beginning of the relationship, each person desires the other as an unique individual who cannot simply be replaced by another person. She says that "the desire felt by two people in love concerns them as individuals; they are unwilling for this to be contradicted by experiences with outsiders; they want each other to be irreplacable for the other...."[50] This is the possessive aspect of erotic love. But the problem arises because of the boredom and the lack of spontaneity present in most marriages. On one hand, each wants to possess the other in an intimate, unique way, but after a long-term relationship the initial joy of spontaneous sex fades into boredom. Yet long after erotic desire is gone, the desire for possession of the other remains. Hence, even if no physical desire remains, neither is typically willing to allow the other the needed freedom for extramarital relations. The erotic is gone from the relation, but the possessive quality of love remains.

Given this situation, de Beauvoir says that what generally happens is that the marriage partners begin to be unfaithful to each other. They seek fulfillment without the consent of their spouse. Hence the institution of marriage creates adultery.[51] The failure of sexual satisfaction within the institution creates the need for deceit and dishonesty. Because a woman has been taught since childhood that her human worth and power exist only if "...she is desirable, lovable (and) if she is desired and loved,"[52] it is only natural that she should go beyond her husband to find this recognition. She must work her magic on someone besides her husband who knows too well that "her magic" is commonplace.

However, if adultery is chosen, it is especially risky for the wife due to the double standard. A woman always has more to lose from being exposed in an adulterous relation. Not only does she lose her standing in the community, but if the affair ends in a divorce, a woman typically loses her means of support. An adulteress is seldom rewarded alimony and, being ill-prepared to earn her own living, the typical woman is in a precarious situation. A man, on the other hand, if caught in adulterous relations, is seldom reprimanded because infidelity is expected of men. If a divorce does ensue, he may be forced to pay some alimony, but he still maintains his financial autonomy. He does not lose his job; the woman on the other hand loses her "job" as "homemaker" and is forced to seek real employment. But because she is seldom well-prepared for the job market and the existing inequalities in pay scales for men and women, a woman's punishment for adultery is much more extreme than the man's.

Given that she is barred from any real action which might provide sexual fulfillment, the frustrated wife may become frigid as a way of punishing her husband. Frigidity is "the spirit of revenge" of the resentful wife. Or, as we have seen, she may spiritualize her frustrations by joining a religion which turns abstinence into a virtue. Or she may overemphasize her role as a mother in hopes of being the least seductive possible. Because motherhood is a virtue, she can disguise her ressentiment in what appears to be the purest of motives. She is socially above reproach.

From our examination of the chapters on the young girl and sexual initiation we know that the woman who enters marriage is typically psychologically ill-equipped for a sexually fulfilling relationship. While marriage does not create the initial psychological problems, it does nothing to solve them, and all too often

creates even more severe problems. This is because of the contradictory roles that the married woman is asked to play. Her problems
are also intensified because of the contradictory notions men
typically have of what a "wife" should be.

The dichotomy is a very simple one. First, as we have seen,
de Beauvoir believes that a woman is typically brought up to believe
that there is something sinful about sexual relations. Yet, on the
other hand, her sexuality is what has been emphasized since
adolescence. Her value and power as a person have been primarily
related to the sexual appeal she has to men; that is, to her ability
to sexually excite the male of the species and hence control him.
And finally, as a human being, she naturally desires sexual fulfillment. Hence we have two approaches to sexuality. Sex is
naturally desired and socially the ground of her value, while at the
same time sex openly pursued is a sin. The classic images that
de Beauvoir employs to illustrate how women, as well as men, deal
with this dichotomy are the chaste "Virgin Mary" on one hand, and
the temptress "Eve" on the other. Or once the woman has children,
the "Virgin Mary" image is simply transformed into the "Mother Mary."

As the "Virgin Mary" woman is expected to be chaste, virtuous,
and a devoted mother. Sex is for the sake of children and is not
to be enjoyed for its own sake. The behaviors that she is taught
as a young girl, the passivity, coquettishness, doll-like behaviors
of the "properly raised" young girl, all make the girl feel guilty
when she begins to act on her natural desires for sexual excitement.

Her proper role as the "Virgin Mary" is to be a devoted mother. Well bred girls do not enjoy sex.

But as a female animal, a woman desires sexual fulfillment. And, much of her early training has given her the idea that her success in life is dependent upon her ability to sexually excite men. To deny this is to deny a part of herself which is essential for social success and natural for her as a female member of the species. To be educated as a temptress and at the same time told that sex is sinful can only result in neurosis or at best some bizarre methods of sublimation. If she is successful as a temptress, she is a sinner by her social and religious standards. If she is the chaste "Virgin Mary," she is frustrated as a human being. In such a contradictory state, it is only natural that sexual fulfillment is made nearly impossible.

As previously mentioned, a woman has many psychological ways of dealing with the problem. According to de Beauvoir, if there is no sexual fulfillment present in the relationship and the woman no longer believes that sex is a man's marital right, then she may deny sexual pleasure to her husband in the name of a higher reality--God. Not only does this turn abstinence into a virtue, but because God is by definition higher and more important than one's husband; one's religious duties clearly take precedence over one's marital duties. Through renouncing the flesh in the name of Christianity a woman can at once spare herself the pain of unsatisfying sexual relations, reap revenge upon her husband for his lack of sexual sensitivity,

and gain a feeling of self-worth through pious devotion to the
church and the Divine.[53]

Turning towards religion is much more natural for women than
for men. De Beauvoir points out that psychologically women are
inclined towards religion not only to reap revenge and belittle
their husbands' power, but because the mystical elements of religion
can be used to squelch man's continual appeal to reason, something
women, lacking the proper training, tend not to understand and
to resent. But within the realm of religion, "Masculine logic is
confronted by the holy mysteries; men's pride becomes a sin; their
agitation for this and that is more than absurd, it is blameworthy:
why remodel this world which God himself created?"[54]

In many ways religion becomes the opium of the frustrated
woman.

> There must be a religion for woman as there must
> be one for the common people, and for exactly the
> same reasons.[55]

Woman's life on earth tends to lack understanding, is painful, and
is frustrating. Religion, as Marx pointed out, justifies this
suffering. "It is the opium of the masses." Woman's spirit of
ressentiment can use the otherwordliness of religion to turn the
pains and frustrations of marriage into virtues. Religion also
makes sure that she does nothing to change her situation. This is
because "the worth of souls is to be weighed only in heaven and not
according to their accomplishments on earth. As Dostoyevsky says,
"here below it is just a matter of different occupations; shining

shoes or building a bridge, all alike is vanity."[56] Hence, such a
perspective both justifies and reinforces a woman's passive stance
toward the world.

One might ask how this troublesome Eve/Virgin Mary dichotomy
arose. Is it totally the effect of the problems inherent in the
traditional institution of marriage? Or are there more fundamental
reasons underlying this bifurcated self-image.[57] Ironically, rather
than the problem arising wholly out of woman's situation, according
to de Beauvoir, it arose out of man's own self-concept as a duality.

In the Greek tradition man was seen as a "fallen God."[58]
Man's own self-concept was that of a godlike being who had been
forced to take on a body and dwell among the animals on earth. As a
fallen god, man was composed of two contradictory parts: a body of
transient flesh burdened with fleshly needs and desires and a soul
which was immortal and desired (or at least was supposed to desire)
eternal truth, beauty, and goodness. Within the soul lies man's
intellect or mind. The mind as rational can comprehend the divine
order or the universe or God. In understanding such universal
truths man realizes his true function: to be like the God that
created him. The body, on the other hand, stands in the way of the
mind's growth towards divine understanding. The desires of the
flesh are desires for "what passeth away." The time and energy
spent on these bodily desires are time and energy taken away from
man's true nature or purpose. Thus the ideal man should desire
earthly or fleshly things as little as possible. In the Christian
tradition, abstinence becomes a virtue for both men and women. St.

Paul endorses marriage for those who cannot abstain. In the Greek tradition, Socrates tells us in the Phaedo that he is looking forward to death so that he can be rid of his troublesome body and get on unencumbered in his search for truth.

The problem for woman is that man, the "noble" rational animal, as an animal naturally desires feminine flesh. In fact, according to de Beauvoir, his primary concern for woman is sexual. Hence, man, this "fallen God," spends much of his time and energy contemplating the feminine form, rather than Plato's "Form of the Good." Given that man, in the Greek tradition, believes that sexual desire is not his true purpose and that he also continually desires the female, he must find a way to justify his desire. His supreme desire for feminine flesh must be rationalized. His self-concept will not permit such a lofty spiritual being to lust without guilt after such transient and earthly pleasures. The desired flesh must be spiritualized or his desire justified by blaming external forces. In an attempt to justify his desire he creates an image of woman as Eve, the evil temptress, siren, and seductress. In so doing he can relieve himself of all blame for his "fall." The desire is not his fault; it is the woman who seduces him. She is the guilty party. She is the evil one.

On the other hand, a man may seek to spiritualize his lust by turning lust into a virtue in disguise. He attempts to see his desire as an altruistic social service. He recognizes that the species must be carried on and that woman is the only means to this "noble end." Man then can convince himself that woman is not mere flesh, but that she is a virtuous noble being, the saintly "Virgin Mary." She can be desired sexually because he has turned his sexual desire into a noble social duty and woman into a saint who will help him do his duty. To desire such a virtuous creature is noble, as long as the desire is for the sake of children, family, and society. In doing this he places her on a pedestal. He has spiritualized his sexuality.

As we have already seen in our discussion of ressentiment, the literature of courtly love is filled with this mode of thinking.[59] In this literature the knight does not see his desire for the lady as sexual, but rather as pure and Platonic. He has not been seduced or lowered himself, but rather is ennobled by the whole experience. De Beauvoir quotes Goethe's Faust to succinctly make this point: "The Eternal Feminine/Beckons us upward."[60] Hence, ironically, the lust for feminine flesh has transformed man himself into a more saintly person.

Once woman is seen as the "Virgin Mary" it is only a short step to seeing her as "Mother Mary," the pure and dutiful mother of Christ. Motherhood then becomes associated with saintliness and purity. It becomes an infinitely worthy activity for women. In this reversal, the downward influence of woman is reversed; she summons man no longer earthward but toward the sky.[61]

The Mother Mary ideal is a noble symbol for woman. She is the intermediary between man and God. She is the "gateway to Heaven." She comforts man, feeds the children, cares for the home. Yet, unfortunately, a man is seldom able to desire woman only for such

noble reasons. In fact, man desires woman primarily as an erotic
object and due to this biological fact will have problems in
treating the same woman as both Mother Mary and Eve. Unhappily such
an ambiguous existence is exactly what is called for in marriage.
De Beauvoir describes the dichotomy of the situation clearly when
she says,

> There is a double demand on man which dooms woman
> to duplicity: he wants the woman to be his and to
> remain foreign to him: he fancies her as at once
> servant and enchantress. But in public he admits
> only the first of these desires; the other is a
> sly demand that he hides in the secrecy of his heart
> and flesh...In the shadows of the night man invites
> woman to sin. But in full daylight he disowns the
> sin and the fair sinner. And the women, themselves
> sinners in the secrecy of bed, are only the more
> passionate in public worship....A Manicheanism is
> introduced into the heart of womankind.[62]

De Beauvoir goes on to say that this dichotomy gives rise to
the eternal popularity of the prostitute. The man who cannot allow
himself to openly desire his "virtuous wife," "the mother of his
children" must satisfy his desires elsewhere, with a prostitute.
Again marriage creates the need for adultery. The situation makes
prostitutes attractive to man, not merely as sexual outlets, but
because prostitutes offer no facade about upholding the "official
virtues" of womankind. There is no duplicity in their nature.
The prostitute is completely honest, while the wife is forced to
hold contradictory values and appears hypocritical.[63] Of course
that is not to say that the man is not equally hypocritical.

The problem for the wife though is more than hypocrisy: the
two roles are physiologically contradictory. As we have already

seen, if the woman becomes pregnant she immediately loses her seductive power. The temptress Eve, whether she desires motherhood or not, becomes wholly the plump, motherly type. The woman is trapped. If she desires sex simply for sexual pleasure, she is perceived as unvirtuous. If she becomes pregnant, she loses her seductive power over her husband. Of course this problem could be avoided through abortion, but de Beauvoir is clear that as a rule men are singularly against the practice. They see women who seek abortions as wholly "disowning feminine values."[64] To condone abortion would be for the man, "the fallen god," to publicly admit that what he desires from woman is merely erotic experience, not the more "noble virtues" of children and family. Man's exhaltations of these values would be seen as the shams they really are.[65]

In summary, man's bifurcated concept of his own self as the "rational animal" leads to the bifurcated idea and treatment of woman. Woman, in response to man's actions, assimilates these contradictory notions. What results is a neurotic state of mind and an inability to achieve sexual satisfaction in marriage for both man and woman.

One can also see that on a more fundamental level the initial dichotomy between man, the rational mind, and man, the animal, is an instance of "bad faith," or an attempt to deny the freedom and change inherent in the "for-itself." Many of the predicates which are normally ascribed to a human's authentic nature (becoming, change, spontaneity, choice, decisiveness, adventuresomeness, transcendence, and creativity) can be seen as more closely related to the animal or erotic side than to the mental. But to emphasize the mental is to emphasize such predicates as being, changelessness, the eternal, universal, or the necessary. To emphasize the mental, to the exclusion of the physical, is to emphasize motives and values which are closely related to being as opposed to becoming, to the in-itself as opposed to the for-itself.

De Beauvoir tells us that part of the duplicity of human nature is to desire to become things. In bad faith, humans attempt to deny their freedom and the responsibility for their actions; they seek to deny the problems which arise from continually having to be in a state of becoming: they fear the contingency of their own existence and the problems of having to create their own meaning for life. To emphasize that which appears to be more stable, more certain, and more closely related to the eternal and changeless, to seek eternal truth and certainty, as given in the Socratic ideal, is to seek to deny the uncertainty of life as lived on the animal level. In this sense, the ideal of the philosophical life as contemplation might be seen as the supreme exercise in bad faith, or as the supreme attempt to be God. In attaining absolute certainty man would finally not have to create reasons for his existence. He could dwell in quiet repose--a thing, "thought thinking thought," but a thing nonetheless.

Erotic love of woman, on the other hand, destroys the quietude of intellectual contemplation. It brings man, "the fallen God," back to earth and reminds him of his animality and mortality. It is uncertainty and adventure as opposed to certitude and assurance. At the same time, erotic desire for woman gives woman a certain power over sovereign man which wounds the 'fallen God's ego.' She takes him away from his staid intellectual or civil life and plunges him into adventure, uncertainty, irrationality, and spontaneity. She makes man dream, write poetry, and sing songs; not do philosophy and science.[66] She makes man emotional and jealous, to the point of sometimes committing murder, not for some high noble ideal, but for the love of a particular existing person. Obviously the person who causes such behavior must be exalted beyond mere fleshly significance in order to justify such behavior.

To live in a continued state of erotic love would be asking too much from a being who by nature desires to be "a thing." The magic of the woman must be dissipated. Her spell over the "rational animal" must be ended. According to de Beauvoir, marriage is an attempt to solve this problem. The temptress is quickly reduced to the level of a domestic servant. The fresh young girl who charmed the man is quickly turned into "a heavy matron or a desiccated hag... The dainty jewel intended to decorate his existence becomes a hateful burden."[67]

But, as we have seen, marriage which was intended to be an institution to socialize eroticism, in reality tends to kill it. Man has regained control and stability at the expense of the erotic, and de Beauvoir believes that if the erotic is to be regained, it is normally done outside of the institution of marriage. Thus if one seeks to find sexual fulfillment, she believes that one should look elsewhere than marriage.

From de Beauvoir's perspective, there is also something misguided for a woman to even try to give meaning to her life through eroticism and sexuality in the first place. The woman who desires recognition through her ability to erotically excite a man faces a number of immediate problems. First, the man typically sees her as an object to be conquered or an adventure upon which to embark upon, and not a free, self-conscious human being. The emphasis that man places on feminine beauty shows that he values her outward objective appearance rather than her inner consciousness or spiritual autonomy. Recognition as a pretty plaything or object is not recognition as an equal human being. Secondly, the man typically desires to dominate the woman in the marital relationship. He does not see her as an equal but as some "thing" to conquer, subjugate, and mould to his liking. De Beauvoir says that:

> woman is par excellence the clay in his hands
> which can be passively worked and shaped... he
> educates her, marks her, sets his imprint upon
> her.[68]

Yet woman is of far greater value than mere clay. A woman is more exciting because the moulding process can go on indefinitely. Woman is a challenge, "treasure, sport, and prey."[69] "A too plastic substance is soon finished and done with, because it is easy to work; but what is precious in woman is that something in her somehow eludes every embrace; thus man is master of a reality all the more

worthy of being mastered in that it is constantly escaping control."[70]
Thirdly, the recognition that is achieved through sexuality is particular and not universal. Erotic love typically has as its object
one unique person, thus the value that one attains from that
relationship is far more limited than the value one attains from
one's relationship to society as a whole or one's peers. De Beauvoir
adds that for man, erotic love is often a mere game or an adventure
quite apart from and secondary to what he considers to be his essential life; his productive life in the polis. This shows that men
tend to recognize the difference between the limited recognition
within the family and the more important civil recognition.[71] But
women in the typical sexual relationship are apt to see sexual
recognition or family recognition as the most important aspects of
their lives. Thus the attitude toward each other in the relationship
is radically different. No reciprocal recognition is achieved.

Thus, from de Beauvoir's perspective, if one is seeking erotic
love one had best look for such experiences outside of the
institution of marriage. The institution turns a spontaneous,
natural desire into a civic duty. It turns what should be freely
given into a duty and a right. It robs the young girl of her
seductive power by turning her into a matron or domestic servant.
It creates a bifurcated image of woman as the temptress or seductress,
while at the same time urging her to play the role of the dutiful,
virtuous little housewife or mother.

It is only natural, given her frustration and disappointment,
that the young bride would turn to the next most obvious course in

her search for recognition and self-fulfillment: she devotes her
energies to her work as a housewife. It is only natural because she
has had far more experience washing, cleaning, and cooking than she
has in sexual matters.

B. The Housewife as Vocation

According to de Beauvoir, society has made the life of a
housewife one of the most accessible roles for a woman to choose.
As a housewife, a woman's life is justified. In fact, traditionally,
if a woman chose not to be a nun, this has been the most acceptable
role. In many instances, having few other possibilities, women
simply chose marriage just so they would have a job.

Since the 19th Century, the home has been given extreme
importance in the lives of most people in Western culture, and
caring for the home has been seen as a noble vocation. In such a
situation, being denied outward expression in the world of real work,
a woman naturally looks to the inner world of her home to find
meaning in her life. Unfortunately, this meaning is seldom found.[72]

As might be expected, de Beauvoir is very critical of the life
of the housewife and the notion that housework is a form of meaningful labor. First, she holds that housework is a clear example of
bad faith. Secondly, she believes that it is a form of alienated
labor in the Marxist sense. And finally, she asserts that women are
wrong to choose this vocation, not only for prudential reasons, but
also for ethical reasons. This is a radical claim which needs
careful examination. As previously noted, many modern feminists see

nothing wrong with a woman choosing to be a housewife and mother, as long as she freely chooses the role.[73]

We have already seen that labor is an important and fundamental concept for de Beauvoir. She argues that all inner potential becomes actual only through labor. Through labor, man

> ...put his power to the test; he set up goals and
> opened up roads towards them; in brief, he found
> self-realization as an existent. To maintain, he
> created; he burst out of the present, he opened
> the future....Man's design is not to repeat himself
> in time: it is to take control of the instant and
> mold the future. It is male activity that in
> creating values has made of existence itself a
> value.[74]

What is important is that it is the activity that becomes the ground of value. Conversely, it is wrong to associate value and self-worth with the mere ownership of the objects of labor. This takes the value away from the creator and places it in the created, the mere thing: a clear form of idolatry. Obviously, this sort of analysis is grounded in Marx' notion of alienated labor. For Marx, one sign of alienated labor is when the object of labor begins to have more importance than the creator of the object. This reversal of values allows those who possess the objects of labor to appear to have a kind of false importance rather than any real importance as creators. Thus according to Marx, the capitalist with vast sums of money can take on the appearance of true worth when in fact he or she does nothing.

> That which exists for me through the medium of
> money, that which I can pay for (i.e., which
> money can buy), that I am, as the possessor of

the money. My own power is as great as the power
of money. The properties of money are my own
(the possessor's) properties and faculties. What
I am and can do is therefore, not at all determined by my individuality.[75]

De Beauvoir sees this illusion, or false consciousness, as a
major problem for housewives. They produce nothing, but by
surrounding themselves in their homes with the pretty objects of
others' labor, they believe themselves to have a proportionate
value.[76] Thus their primary role is the acquisition, protection,
and maintenance of objects of labor. The housewife's value is seen
as directly proportional to the value of the house she orders and
cleans.

This too can be seen as another instance of bad faith. The
housewife's role as preserver of her acquired objects denies her
truly human side which should include transcendence and creative
labor, while she identifies herself with her possessions--
possessions she has neither made nor earned. As de Beauvoir says,
"Because she does nothing, she eagerly seeks self-realization in
what she has."[77]

Such an act of bad faith is especially evident in the typical
reception or afternoon club-meeting popular among bourgeois housewives. At the reception "The hostess displays her treasures:
silver, linen, glassware."[78] The greater their worth, the greater
her worth. De Beauvoir sees the epitome of such an attitude in the
women of the upper class, who, because of their wealth, do not even
engage in housework. They live off the exploits of their husbands;

they are but parasites on society and are lost in self-deception.
They are parasites living off of parasites. Because they do
absolutely nothing,

> They repress all thought, all critical judgment,
> all spontaneous impulses; they parrot accepted
> opinions, they confuse with the ideal whatever the
> masculine code imposes on them; all genuineness is
> dead in their heart and even in their faces. (They)
> give nothing, do nothing, in exchange for all they
> get; on this account they believe in the indefeasible
> rights with so much the blinder faith. Their vain
> arrogance, their radical incapability, their
> obstinate ignorance, make them the most useless
> non-entities ever produced by the human species.[79]

The fashionable dress of these women is also an indication of
bad faith. Not only do they tend to equate their human worth with
the stylishness of their clothes, such women attempt literally to
turn themselves into beautiful objects not different from the
exquisite objects with which they surround themselves. "Since
woman is an object, it is quite understandable that her intrinsic
value is affected by her style of dress and adornment...the better
showing a woman makes, the more she is respected...not only does
the woman of fashion project herself into things, she has chosen
to make herself a thing."[80] Their thing-like or "doll-like"
appearance is their way of seeking recognition from others. By
means of adornment, the housewife "who is deprived of doing anything
feels she expresses what she is."[81] But in this very attempt such
women have denied the truly human side of themselves. They have
negated all true creativity, their rational development, and the
ability to transcend their own contingency through meaningful labor.

For housewives, life itself becomes the enemy of all that
they value. Not only does life slowly erode and destroy those
valued objects of their beautiful homes, but life is the enemy
to their own beauty.

> Horror at the depreciation that all living growth
> entails will arouse in certain frigid or frustrated
> women a horror of life itself. They endeavor to
> preserve themselves as others preserve furniture
> or canned food. This negative obstinacy makes them
> enemies of their own existence. She would like to
> shield herself from men, from the world, from time,
> as one protects the furniture with slip-covers.[82]

If the young woman desires to marry a "successful" man in order to
attain this short of sheltered life, her project is self-defeating.
Her life itself is the denial of life. Of course, one might ask
if de Beauvoir has not overlooked the training, culture, and
education that typically accompanies the youthful years of such
women. Why is the self-conscious narcissism necessary for "a
woman of cultured beauty" any more degrading or stultifying than the
project of the young male who goes to college to learn to be a
salesman, and in so doing learns to appear "well-heeled" and
cultured, equipped with all of the social graces needed to sell
his product to a consumer? She sells herself to successful men;
he sells a product to successful people. Is there a fundamental
difference? One major difference is that a woman who is nothing
but a housewife is totally dependent upon her husband for financial
support. A man's training allows him to change jobs with relative
ease, at least in times of economic prosperity. The woman is
trapped.

Of course what de Beauvoir has been discussing is an ideal case rather than the typical. Most women, although they may ultimately desire the success of the wealthy housewife, are not afforded such luxuries. For the majority of women, to be a housewife means to stay home doing the cooking, cleaning, washing, ironing, and caring for the children. Such a life might be seen as more of a job than a "social position." What are the problems with this sort of life?

We have seen that de Beauvoir holds a Marxist's ideal concerning meaningful labor and human development. Her ideal includes such virtues as creativity, critical and logical development, self-transcendence and freely chosen projects which are directed towards higher ends, ends which are invented by the creative mind placed in a world far from ideal, a mind which revolts against the shortcomings of the status quo and posits a new world to be created through labor. For de Beauvoir these loftiest human attitudes such as "heroism, revolt, disinterestedness, imagination, (and) creation,"[83] are seldom present in a housewife. This is simply because the role of a housewife does not force women to develop these capacities. As we have seen, a woman's development along these ideal lines has been systematically thwarted since childhood. How, according to de Beauvoir, does the work of a normal housewife continue this stultification? Besides losing one's true identity through the objects of labor, how is this role an instance of alienated labor?

First of all, de Beauvoir considers housework a non-productive activity. Cleaning the house is a routine, much like Sisyphus and his rock, which is endlessly repeated with no true end or goal beyond the activity of maintaining the status quo. To keep the house orderly is an endless battle against the natural forces of life, dirt, and the effects of normal human activities. (De Beauvoir does not believe this female Sisyphus to be happy!) "It is really too bad to have husband and children trample with muddy feet all over her waxed hardwood floors."[84] It is unfortunate that the cake, "nearly too pretty to eat," will soon be consumed and destroyed. De Beauvoir's point is that the end or telos of domestic work is merely a continued repetition of the same activity. This is because the products of domestic work have no enduring value but must be continuously consumed.

The act of labor that goes into maintaining the home is itself for the most part mindless and repetitive. It is work which could easily be done by a robot. The activity develops no creativity or individuality; it could be done by anyone. According to de Beauvoir, the housewive's days are "a gilded mediocrity lacking ambition and passion, aimless days infinitely repeated, life that slips away towards death without ever questioning its purpose -- that is what they mean by happiness."[85] Washing, ironing, sweeping, cooking, ad nauseum. As Marx would say, when engaged in such alienated labor, a person

> ...does not fulfill himself in his work but denies
> himself, has a feeling of misery rather than well

> being, does not develop freely his mental and
> physical energies but is physically exhausted and
> mentally debased...It is not a satisfaction of a
> need, but only a <u>means</u> for satisfying other
> needs...it is not <u>his</u> own work but work for some-
> one else...the activity is not his own spontaneous
> activity.[86]

For all practical purposes, housework is not the woman's own;
it too belongs to another. Typically, the woman is literally
employed by her husband. Through her stultifying labor, she denies
her true human development so that her husband can develop his
capacities through labor in the world. (Of course this presupposes
that the man is not also involved in some equally meaningless and
stultifying task.)

Why would any woman choose such a life? What are the reinforcers? De Beauvoir believes that the reward of such labor is
vicariously obtained through the romanticization of a housewife by
the husband. A kind of false-consciousness is developed. The
husband commends the wife for a good meal and is proud of the clean-
liness and orderliness of his home after returning from the world of
work. Men also idealize the life of the housewife by pointing out
how free she is in staying home with her work, while he has to go
out into the hard cruel world to make a living. But from de
Beauvoir's perspective such freedom is empty.[87] The housewife is
free, but free to do nothing.

This idealization or mystification of the life of a housewife
is one of the ways for man to retain his superiority and control
of women. The husband, by making a living, has made his house-
keeper/wife tremendously dependent upon him. In keeping her at home

and making sure the only skills she has are domestic skills, he has prevented her from ever choosing to divorce him. If the wife were to confront her husband, he would remind her very quickly that if it were not for him, she would starve to death. In her dependent state, she is forced to extol the virtues of her wonderful provider. Like a slave, she is forced to feel grateful to her "master." She has sold her life to her husband as Marx says the wage laborer sells his life to the bourgeoisie. In that sense, she is estranged from her husband as the worker is from the capitalist.[88]

But ironically. in limiting her to the endless, stultifying, mechanical labor of housework, the husband can at the same time be assured that his wife will not develop any truly human potentials. Two things follow from this: first, the wife, who for all practical concerns does nothing, is nothing. Thus she is a boring companion for his treasured leisure hours after work. This inclines the "loving and protective" husband towards evening social functions or adultery in some cases, as attempts to escape from his boring wife and the 'wonderful' home she provides. Secondly, the wife, being denied her natural development, may become resentful and find subtle ways to punish her husband. As we have seen, such ways include sexual frigidity, shrewish behavior, time consuming involvement with religious groups, spending beyond the budget, or making the husband wait when they have a social engagement. All of these "typically feminine" activities are subtle forms of ressentiment and revenge.

Although husbands would lose a good deal of their control over their wives, ironically their wives would be infinitely more interesting persons if they were allowed to go out into the world and fulfill themselves through meaningful labor. Thus again with a typical dialectical inversion, the traditional marriage and the vocation of housekeeper by the wife not only enslaves the woman, but in the end, according to de Beauvoir, destroys the freedom and happiness of the man--the master.

> The dialectic of the master and slave here finds its
> most concrete expression: in oppressing, one
> becomes oppressed. Men are enchained by reason of
> their very sovereignty. It is because they alone
> earn money that their wives demand checks; it is
> because they alone engage in a business or profession
> that their wives require them to be successful, it is
> because they alone embody transcendence that their
> wives wish to rob them of it by taking charge of
> their projects and successes.[89]

The bored frustrated housewife, alienated in her work and from the world in general, takes her revenge out on her husband who ironically keeps her in that oppressed state. The image of the nagging shrewish wife is not a statement about feminine nature, rather it is a symptom of the malaise which underlies the traditional institution of marriage. Housewives are shewish precisely because "marriage makes women into 'praying mantisses,' 'leeches,' 'poisonous creatures' and so on...Woman leans heavily on man because she is not allowed to rely on herself; he will free himself in freeing her--that is to say, in giving her something to do in the world."[90]

One might argue that woman's life in the home may be boring and personally stultifying, but there is one aspect of Marx's notion of alienated labor which is missing: competition with and alienation from one's fellow workers. In this sense it appears that women could form much closer relationships with their "fellow workers" than men. De Beauvoir does on occasion recognize the special closeness of female friendships. She recognizes that there is a certain collegiality between women as there is among all oppressed classes. "Women's mutual understanding comes from the fact that they identify themselves with each other...A housewife has more intimate relations with her maid than any man...ever has with his valet...Women are comrades in captivity for one another; they help one another endure their prison."[91] A man must go out and compete in the "dog eat dog world." Each fellow worker is a threat to his job security or chances for promotion. A woman on the other hand has the security of the home and need not see other women as threats to that security. Truly human friendships, far beyond mere utility, may be formed between women. Thus it could be argued that a woman's labor in the home is not truly alienated labor in the Marxian sense because she does not compete with others. What she loses in boredom and self-mortification, she gains through self-fulfilling friendship. A man, on the other hand, may be involved in meaningful labor, but he is alienated from his fellow workers.

In spite of such an argument, de Beauvoir argues that the social relations between housewives are not truly human and that

there is nearly as much competition between housewives as between
businessmen. Her analysis takes the following form: a true
friendship is a relationship where "ideas and projects of a personal
interest are discussed."[92] Each is genuinely concerned and
interested in the work of the other in its individuality. There is
no threat from the other to one's position or merit as a person.
A kind of genuineness and reciprocity is at work between each member
where each not only allows the other to achieve self-fulfillment,
but aids the process whenever possible. Such relationships are rare
among persons, but even rarer among women. Why is this?

First of all, according to de Beauvoir, women generally have
little to give in a relationship. Their realm of experience is so
limited and their interest or understanding of the world beyond
home and family so meager, that all too frequently they have nothing
to say to each other. "Their correspondence deals especially with
beauty counsel, recipes for cooking, directions for knitting."[93]
Their gatherings are typical instances of what Heidegger called
"idle talk."

Secondly, there is a kind of competition going on even between
housewives, much like that which exists between workers. Each seeks
to impress the other with her "things" or her beauty, as these are
her signs of being successful. Each new acquisition of home or
furniture by one of her fellow housewives is seen as a threat to
her relative status or worth in the social community. A new dress
which beautifies a friend turns that person into a threat for her

own worth as a sexual object. De Beauvoir believes that the games played by women in society are every bit as cunning as those played by male competitors in the marketplace. Yet unlike most men, woman is unusually aware of the fact that she knows that others could perform the function as well as she could.[94] Thus the other is always a threat to her security as the other could easily replace her. When the housewife is honest she recognizes that there is nothing unique about cleaning house, ironing clothes, and following a recipe in a cookbook. Any other person could do these tasks equally as well.

Also, if the housewife happens to love her husband, a rare occurrence in itself according to de Beauvoir, the close friend is a supreme threat because the friend will know all of the virtues of the husband as told by the wife, and at the same time see all of the wife's weaknesses. This makes the wife very vulnerable if the friend should desire an affair with her husband.[95]

Finally, a housewife sees that her life is dependent upon her husband. Her first allegiance is always toward the person who benefits her the most. Friendships between women typically result in sessions of open complaints about their plights, but this relationship becomes secondary once the husband asks for allegiance to him.

We have seen how de Beauvoir criticizes housework as a kind of bad faith in that a housewife seeks to lose herself in the objects with which she surrounds herself. She loses herself in the role and the objects which accompany the role. In the same sense, she is alienated from the objects. The objects, the house, the furniture, etc., enslave her. Even though she acquires them in an attempt to give her life meaning, once she owns all of the bric a brac she must spend hours cleaning and preserving their beauty. This house-work is also seen as an example of being alienated from the act of labor due to its repetitive, stultifying nature. The labor is in reality not hers but is forced upon her by her husband. It is forced because the husband will not support her unless she does her duty. And finally, we have seen that de Beauvoir sees housewives as alienated from their fellow workers. And, like Marx, who saw that in such a state both workers and capitalists were alienated, de Beauvoir sees that the traditional situation enslaves both the husband and the wife. And, like Marx, her solution to overcome the alienation between husband and wife is for both to attain a kind of equality through both engaging in meaningful labor.

Her final criticism of a woman choosing the life of a house-wife goes beyond the prudential concerns over the effects that such a life has on the husband and the wife. The criticism deals with the effects the role of housewife and mother has on the children in such a marriage. The argument takes on a moral tone as it is not so much concerned with the consequences for each housewife, but rather with how taking on such a role harms others. The woman may choose to ignore her own well being, but that does not mean that she has a right to ignore the well-being of her children.

De Beauvoir's concern for the education of children is no
less than that of Plato's in his Republic.[96] Both see that the
future of a people lies in the hands of the children and that if
those children are not properly raised and educated, the future
will be tainted with their inadequacies. Both also see that
children develop many of their attitudes and values by imitating
their parents. Thus the role that the parent acts out before the
eyes of the young child is very important in terms of the later
development of the child. Both argue that if the role does not
benefit the child or the society, the parent should not engage in
the behavior.

As we have seen, de Beauvoir is very clear in her chapter on
early childhood that one of the primary reasons female children fail
to develop their rational and creative capacities is because they
imitate their mothers, and the kinds of activities involved in the
mother's role as a housewife are not the kinds of behaviors which
develop one's capacities. Secondly, after her analysis of housework,
there is a further problem: a housewife is frustrated, bored,
oppressed, and generally unhappy. Because of her psychological
state of resentment, she is inclined to take out her frustrations
on the child. De Beauvoir's concern over this is obvious.

> The great danger which threatens the infant in our
> culture lies in the fact that the mother to whom
> it is confided in all its helplessness is almost
> always a discontented woman: sexually she feels
> herself inferior to man; she has no independent grasp
> on the world or on the future. She will seek to
> compensate for all these frustrations through her

> child. When it is realized how difficult woman's
> present situation makes her full self-realization,
> ...one is frightened at the thought that defense-
> less infants are abandoned to her care.[97]

Thus the question of whether or not to become a housewife is a question that goes beyond mere concerns for one's own well-being. It is a question that has important consequences for others; i.e., our children. A housewife, according to de Beauvoir, simply makes a poor mother. Conversely, "the woman who enjoys the richest individual life will have the most to give to her children and will demand least from them; she who acquires in effort and struggle a sense of true human values will be best able to bring them up properly."[98]

The discussion of the problems with the life of the housewife/ mother will be continued in our next section on motherhood. Let it suffice for now to say that the importance of children and how they grow up cannot be overemphasized for any radical thinker like de Beauvoir. If the structure of the society and its values are going to change, the change can best be achieved through educating the naive mind of the child. In the same sense, if one desires to maintain the status quo there is no easier way than to firmly ingrain in the mind of the child through example and education that what is, is right. If the roles of women are going to change, the models that the children imitate must change.

C. Motherhood as a Means to Social Recognition and
   Self-Fulfillment

Sexually frustrated, isolated from society, tired of the
repetitive stultifying round of household duties, a woman more and
more desperately desires the satisfaction that marriage has
promised. Her most immediate and natural option which might transform the current abysmal situation is for her to have a child. To
have a child is to achieve at once social recognition, human
relationship to overcome her loneliness, and a way of making her
life less boring.

To have a child is to attain a degree of social worth. Society
had traditionally reinforced motherhood. It has been the easiest
way for woman to achieve a kind of hallowed status, as well as
social esteem.[99] Motherhood is seen as woman's unique service to
the state; otherwise, a woman is looked at as "so much wastage."[100]
Thus, in any society where children are valued, motherhood is an
esteemed profession. Yet ironically no matter how highly a state
values the woman's services for providing consumers and "cannon
fodder," the state never pays the mother for her profession the way
it pays other workers. Yet even without pay for her services, a
woman who becomes a mother manages to feel that she has some social
worth. This is probably related to the fact that other opportunities
for recognition were denied until fairly recently.

The problem with this is simply that if a woman's social value
and self-respect are intimately tied to her biological function of
reproducing the species, it is easy to see how depressed and worthless

a woman might feel if she were barren or once the children that she has brought into the world have left the home. As her children leave, so does her raison d'etre.[101]

Secondly, de Beauvoir points out that what the woman seeks in the child is self-recognition from another self-conscious autonomous being. But, the child, who is at first thought to be such a being, turns out in reality not able to provide the desired recognition and interaction.[102] The baby, rather than providing the needed intellectual stimulation, merely smiles and babbles. There is no equality in the relation. And finally, if a mother views her child as a product of her labor to be compared with other products, ironically the child's unique value as an individual is determined solely by the mother, not by any real socially recognized standard. To be mother is not to be an artist.

Hence, de Beauvoir believes that the woman who desires marriage for the sake of children is involved in a project that can only end in disappointment and frustration. Not only is the needed reciprocity between mother and child missing, but pregnancy and motherhood are poor excuses for real "human" creativity. In real creative labor there is first the initial idea or plan which is freely conceived and then there is the human activity of consciously bringing the idea into reality. This realization is through labor. In the case of motherhood, however, the woman is passive. Once impregnated, the process proceeds unconsciously. She does not create the child; the child creates itself. Nature takes its course.

Secondly, whereas in real creativity the talent possessed by the individual is unique, the mother's creative power is nothing unique but is common to the whole of the female sex. Thus from this perspective, there is no real analogy between authentic human labor and the woman's creating a child in her womb. The woman submits "passively to her biologic fate!"[103] From submitting to this biological process the mother should feel but little pride, nor does she realize any truly human potential through a process which is common to all animals. Her human value is reduced to an animal function.

De Beauvoir does not argue that in all instances choosing to be a mother is wrong or unfulfilling. Rather she argues that many women typically get married in order to have "a family" and desire this for all the wrong reasons. Because of their situation of being isolated, they desire children in order to have someone to whom to relate. But, according to de Beauvoir, for a woman to desire children out of lack or her own life of emptiness is wrong. The desired personal fulfillment and social recognition will not be forthcoming. Simply because a woman might suffer from the neurosis of a stultified childhood or empty marriage or loneliness is not a sufficient reason for desiring children. De Beauvoir says that "it is criminal to recommend having a child as a remedy for melancholia or neurosis; that means unhappiness of both mother and child."[104] It is wrong to substitute children for one's own disappointing life. The child can never fill the void in an adult life with adult needs.

On this point, de Beauvoir's position on marriage and motherhood is very close to Nietzsche's position in Thus Spoke Zarathustra
where Zarathustra speaks "On Child and Marriage." There Nietzsche
asks,

> Are you a man entitled to wish for a child? Are you
> a victorious one, the self conqueror, the commander
> of your senses, the master of your virtues. This I
> ask you? Or is it the animal and need that speak out
> of your wish? Or loneliness, or lack of peace with
> yourself? Let your victory and your freedom long for
> a child. You shall bring living monuments to your
> victory and your liberation. You shall build over
> and beyond yourself, but first you must be built
> yourself...You shall not only reproduce yourself,
> but product something higher.[105]

Not out of weakness and need should a woman desire a child,
but rather out of strength and the desire to create. De Beauvoir
says that "only the woman who is well balanced, healthy, and aware
of her responsibilities is capable of being a good mother...She
cannot consent to bring forth life unless life has meaning."[106]
This meaning that she holds in such high regard is only achieved
through meaningful labor, not through biological reproduction.

As we have already seen, not only does the child not fulfill
the mother's needs; but the unfulfilled woman does not fulfill the
child's needs. "The great danger which threatens the infant in our
culture lies in the fact that the mother to whom it is confided in
all its helplessness is almost always a discontented woman."[107]
From this de Beauvoir concludes that the best mothers will be those
who work, who already have a high degree of self-esteem, who have
already realized some of their concrete human potentials, understand

the world in some rational way, and can impart this understanding to the child. Ironically, such an argument may entail that the best mothers in our present society would be men. She summarizes her position clearly in a 1972 interview when she says, "...women will not be liberated until they are liberated from children, and children are at the same time to some degree liberated from adults."[108] In this sense the sins of the mother are imparted to the child. The mother's frustrations and unhappiness are placed upon the child's shoulders, shoulders far too small to carry such a burden.

Yet another problem with seeking values through motherhood is that there is a basic contradiction between a woman's value qua beautiful object and the physical changes which accompany pregnancy.[109] As we have seen, a young girl's training early in her life teaches her that her value as a woman is directly related to her beauty, particularly the shapeliness of her figure. To desire children in order to give one's life meaning contradicts this initial desire to be beautiful. Pregnancy, at least temporarily and sometimes permanently, destroys the woman's beauty and hence negates her power over men. Once she is pregnant, her limited power over men is inversely proportional to the thickening of her waist. Because of this, de Beauvoir holds that women often experience extreme horror at seeing their once beautiful bodies change and because of this tend to resent the child.[110] The fetus, which was first to be their salvation from a lonely, meaningless life, is now its enemy. Because of the ambiguity of the situation, it is hard to truly love and rejoice over the presence of this enemy within.

Finally, and perhaps most importantly, because de Beauvoir holds that authentic self-development occurs only through meaningful labor, motherhood is an enemy to a woman's true self-fulfillment simply because caring for the child tends to keep her at home rather than allowing her to go out into the society and work.

Not only does the child keep the mother at home, denying her access to the working world, keeping her in relative isolation from other human beings (except perhaps other oppressed housewives), but the situation insures that she will remain economically dependent on her husband. And if the marriage ends in divorce, and she is awarded the children, as is usually the case, her marketability as a future wife is supremely limited. In all cases, the child limits the woman's freedom even more.

The arguments against motherhood could be seen merely as arguments which show that it is not in the woman's self-interest to be a mother. This would turn de Beauvoir's feminism into a kind of egoism. But when we remember that de Beauvoir believes that the situation is ultimately harmful to the child, then her position becomes one of concern for others rather than merely for one's self. It is because the mother's frustration typically ends up in revenge on the child that motherhood is a potentially selfish and exploitive vocation for the mother. The child is being used.

Another point that is extremely important is that the woman's
revenge may take the form of making sure that any female child ends
up like the mother, or that a male child is given his model for
feminine behavior in terms of an unhappy, lonely, frustrated mother.
The mother's role thus becomes perpetuated into the next genera-
tion.[111] The problem of the mother providing an improper model for
her children is the core of her argument as to why "No woman should
be authorized to stay at home to raise her children."[112]

When a woman does make such a choice, and her education and
the society make the choice very appealing, she is condemning
herself to a life of immanence, frustration, and boredom.

VI. The Working Woman

After all that de Beauvoir has said about the value of labor,
the need for economic independence, and the self-esteem which
accompanies economic freedom, one might suspect that all of a woman's
problems will be solved once she moves beyond the immanent, passive
existence as a housewife/mother and takes on the active role as a
wage-earner. Such is not the case.

It is true that de Beauvoir believes that economic freedom is
the foundation of all other freedoms. For her, civil liberties
remain theoretical for a woman who is still a parasite within the
traditional system.[113] Woman's escape from oppression by man
must be through her labor and economic independence. Unfortunately,
according to de Beauvoir, "working today is not liberty."[114] The

promised freedom and self-fulfillment are seldom found. Let us examine the reasons for this.

First, the woman who works is usually engaged in some kind of labor in the world which is equally as oppressive and repetitious as housework. Second, not only are women given bad jobs, but they receive poor pay.[115] There are obvious reasons for this. First, women are ill-equipped to enter the world of work due to their childhood and their education. Second, women typically take on jobs as "pin money," or merely to supplement their husband's income.[116] Thus it is not necessary for the employer to pay them even "a subsistence wage." This assures that a woman, unless she is a "professional" of some sort, will still remain dependent upon her husband. De Beauvoir claims that the job situation for most working women is so grim that in order to continue they must be political visionaries who envision what women's future life might be like in order to put up with current working conditions and low pay.[117] An added complication to receiving low pay for unfulfilling work is that the choice for women is usually not whether to work or be a housewife. In reality the choice is whether to work and be a housewife, or to be only a housewife. To choose to work is to take on a second job. The traditional husband, with his manly self-image, is usually not willing to take over his share of the household duties. Hence the woman is expected to work forty hours at a job and then go home and work at a second job of cleaning, washing, ironing, cooking, etc.[118]

Given such a situation it is no wonder that women choose to remain housewives, even though this choice assures them that they will forever remain economically dependent upon their husbands, which in turn will make them always unequal in all facets of their relationship. And the irony is that given the mystification which surrounds the vocation of a housewife-mother, coupled with the problems which confront the woman who chooses to go to work, the housewife will feel herself lucky to be taken care of by her huband. This is why de Beauvoir says that women's emancipation is contingent upon doing away with this choice of remaining a housewife. As long as it is an option, because of its appeal when compared to the other options, large numbers of women will choose it and hence the situation which insures inequality and oppression will continue.[119]

The effects of the option of being a housewife affects all aspects of the woman's life and training (or lack of it). For example, the possibility of justifying one's existence through becoming a housewife, rather than the woman knowing that she will have to care for herself in the world, has a great effect on the young girl's attitude toward education.[120] The young girl knows that the option of being taken care of is always present, and this prevents her "from unreservedly applying herself to her studies and her career."[121] When she does not apply herself, she soon convinces herself that she cannot understand the subject matter at hand. This soon leads her to believe that she is inferior and that "Boys are better than girls, they are better workers."[122] It is not "penis

envy" as Freud thought. The effect of this is that she ends up
ill-prepared for any career, other than that of a housewife. Her
feelings of inferiority and the passivity of "feminine behavior"
which have been reinforced since her childhood, make her a poor match
for the competitive, self-assertive spirit of the male in the
working place.

Hence, according to de Beauvoir, most of the harmful behavior
which young girls adopt is a function of allowing them the option
of choosing to be housewives. They do not develop the skills
necessary to be independent transcendent persons simply because they
know they do not have to; they believe that in the end some man
will always take care of them. All human beings, according to de
Beauvoir, have such a tendency towards immanence. All in bad faith
seek to deny their freedom, to pull back from responsibility and
transcendence and become things. However, the difference between
male and female character is that transcendence is <u>demanded</u> of the
male and not of the female. The female can always choose to be a
housewife.

One might argue that if the working world were more inviting,
with changes in labor laws and if husbands ceased believing that
only women do housework, perhaps more women would choose to be as
independent as possible and prepare themselves for a career beyond
the home. This is the attitude of many contemporary feminists. But
according to de Beauvoir, such social changes and positive reinforcers
are not enough. Even if a woman is serious about her career, she

will not be as dedicated to absolute success as a man is. As long as the choice to be a housewife remains, a woman knows that if she fails or is only mediocre, she will always be taken care of. Second, the childhood of young girls must be changed. A woman's childhood has not prepared her for the business world. Women are typically trained to be passive objects concerned primarily with their appearance. This narcissism and concern for appearances makes a young girl more interested in appearing to be a success than in being a success. Or, later in life, de Beauvoir holds that women are more interested in success per se than getting serious about mastering the means to success.[123] Caught up in herself, woman cannot transcend the present with its focus on herself. As de Beauvoir so succinctly states the problem, "What woman essentially lacks today for doing great things is forgetfulness of herself; but to forget oneself it is first of all necessary to be firmly assured that now and for the future, one has found oneself."[124]

If such personality problems were not enough, de Beauvoir points out that women also encounter problems in working with men and (ironically) with other women. Obviously men will have trouble working with women, especially if the woman is of an equal or superior rank. First of all, men do not know whether to treat a woman as a sex object to be conquered or as a colleague. Likewise, the woman doesn't know whether to do everything in her power to renounce her feminity or to behave as she always has, as a sex object. She is divided against herself.

Secondly, men also will have trouble treating women as equals; given that it is traditionally believed that women are inferior. And because a woman has been "reared in an atmosphere of respect for male superiority,"[125] she will have trouble asserting herself in her position. Because of her childhood, she will always tend to feel inferior to her male colleagues, no matter what her rank.

Her relation with other women is equally perilous. As a class, women in the working world have justified their mediocre success in terms of being women. If one believes that women are by nature inferior, then if one fails, the responsibility for failure is not one's own. The responsibility lies in the fact that one is "a woman," a fact beyond one's control. But, as de Beauvoir points out, if some women do become relatively successful in the working world, these counter examples to women's traditional rationalization for failure make other women very resentful of the successful woman.[126] Such resentful women, convinced of their own natural inferiority, will always be more supportive of their male superior than of a woman who has risen above them. Lacking the support of other female employees makes the continued success of a female executive, administrator, or manager very difficult.

If the fundamental problem limiting women's freedom is inequality and the basic inequality is economic, but the working environment, coupled with their lack of preparation, makes their success in the working world unlikely, what then is to be done? Unless some solution is suggested The Second Sex becomes a totally pessimistic

book. If what is essential for women to attain equality comes

down to achieving economic equality and given de Beauvoir's analysis

of the world of work for women, it appears that women will never

be equal to men.

However, I believe that de Beauvoir does offer a solution in

a number of places in the book. Her solution is that the economic

system must become socialist, and within such a system, girls

must be raised exactly like boys. Thus according to de Beauvoir,

the liberation of women and the liberation of the proletariat are

closely linked. This is obvious from what she says in her chapter

criticizing the determinism of some version of historical

materialism,

> ...it is this economic oppression that gives rise to
> the social oppression to which she is subjected.
> Equality cannot be re-established until the two sexes
> enjoy equal rights by law; but this enfranchisement
> requires participation in general industry by the
> whole female sex...It is the resistance of the ancient
> capitalistic paternalism that in most countries
> prevents the concrete realization of this equality:
> it will be realized on the day when this resistance
> is broken....127

Later in her chapter on women since the French Revolution she

echoes this same belief. "When economic power falls into the hands

of the workers, then it will be possible for the working woman to

win rights and privileges that the parasitic woman, noble or

middle-class, has never attained."[128] And finally in her final

chapter on the working woman she says, "...working today is not

130

liberty. Only in a socialist world would woman by the one attain the other."[129]

One might ask why de Beauvoir emphasizes socialism. How is socialism linked to women's liberation? Simply put, for de Beauvoir, socialism would at least in principle create a world where men and women were equal, where "women raised and trained exactly like men were to work under the same conditions and for the same wages...woman was to be obliged to provide herself with other ways of earning a living..." besides being a housewife.[130] Pregnancy would not present a problem because the state would pay for pregnancy leaves and for child-care.[131]

In such a situation a girl would be raised as a boy because a woman's role would be like a man's in the society. The option of being a housewife/mother would be missing. Hence all the behaviors which are developed by women to catch a man to support them would be nonexistent. They would be forced to be free. They would be freed for independence and self-sufficiency. Love between people would be based on emotion, not on fiscal need.

FOOTNOTES

[1]SS 301.

[2]SS 302.

[3]SS 303.

[4]Ibid.

[5]SS 305.

[6]SS 310.

[7]The resemblance between de Beauvoir's description and Rousseau's in his Emilius' or A New System of Education is remarkable. The difference is that Rousseau accepts all of this as natural, while de Beauvoir is very critical of this traditional childhood role and the values which it embodies. See Woman in Western Thought, ed. Martha Lee Osborne (New York: Random House, 1979), pp. 107-121.

[8]SS 316.

[9]SS 318.

[10]SS 320-321.

[11]SS 336.

[12]SS 334.

[13]SS 336.

[14]SS 316.

[15]Ibid.

[16]SS 330, 332, 336.

[17]SS 368.

[18]SS 369.

[19]Ibid.

[20]SS 370.

[21]Ibid.

[22]SS 371.

[23]SS 376.

[24]SS 378.

[25]SS 383.

[26]SS 386.

[27]SS 459, 470.

[28]SS 388.

[29]SS 392.

[30]SS 413.

[31]SS 437.

[32]SS 439.

[33]SS 438.

[34]SS 448.

[35]As I previously noted we will skip the chapter on lesbians, noting only that from de Beauvoir's perspective it makes perfectly good sense for a woman to choose a lesbian relation given the difficulties of heterosexual relations just outlined.

[36]SS 175.

[37] _SS_ 482.

[38] _SS_ 481.

[39] _SS_ 436.

[40] _SS_ 491.

[41] _SS_ 448.

[42] _SS_ 479.

[43] _SS_ 481.

[44] _SS_ 488.

[45] _SS_ 185.

[46] _SS_ 494.

[47] _SS_ 495.

[48] _SS_ 497.

[49] _SS_ 498.

[50] _Ibid._

[51] _SS_ 212.

[52] _SS_ 610.

[53] _SS_ 192-194.

[54] _SS_ 692.

[55] _SS_ 691.

[56] _Ibid._

134

⁵⁷For an excellent discussion of the many manifestations of
woman as the Virgin and the Earth Mother throughout the history
of religion see Rosemary Ruether's book <u>New Woman/New Earth</u>,
Seabury Press, 1975. While Ruether does not dwell on the contradictory self-concept that women derive from the Eve/Virgin Mary
dichotomy, her discussion of the significance of the virgin
birth is enlightening. Only in a religion which saw sin as
associated with the human body (and consequently sex) would place
so much emphasis upon its redeemer being immaculately conceived,
born of a virgin. pp. 36-59.

⁵⁸<u>SS</u> 164.

⁵⁹Andraes Cappelanus, <u>The Art of Courtly Love</u>, Trans. John
Jay Parry (New York: Ungar Publishing, 1957).

⁶⁰<u>SS</u> 203.

⁶¹<u>Ibid</u>.

⁶²<u>SS</u> 215-216.

⁶³<u>SS</u> 218-219.

⁶⁴<u>SS</u> 548.

⁶⁵<u>SS</u> 548-549.

⁶⁶<u>SS</u> 208-212.

⁶⁷<u>SS</u> 211-212.

⁶⁸<u>SS</u> 199.

⁶⁹<u>SS</u> 210.

⁷⁰<u>SS</u> 199.

⁷¹<u>SS</u> 682.

⁷²<u>SS</u> 503.

[73]See Alison Jaggar, "Political Philosophies of Women's Liberation," Philosophy and Women, eds. Sharon Bishop and Marjorie Weinzweig (Belmont: Wadsworth Publishing Company, 1979), p. 289.

[74]SS 71, 74.

[75]Marx, Economic and Philosophical Manuscripts, p. 81.

[76]SS 672.

[77]SS 501.

[78]SS 601.

[79]SS 697-698.

[80]SS 595-598.

[81]SS 589.

[82]SS 599.

[83]SS 694.

[84]SS 508.

[85]SS 500.

[86]Marx, Economic and Philosophical Manuscripts, p. 60.

[87]SS 801.

[88]Marx, op. cit., p. 60.

[89]SS 538.

[90]SS 539.

136

[91]SS 606-608.

[92]SS 604.

[93]SS 605.

[94]SS 607.

[95]Ibid.

[96]Plato, Republic, Bks. II, III, IV; see also Helen John, "The Promise of Freedom in the Thought of Simone de Beauvoir: How an infant smiles." Proceedings of the Catholic Phil. Assoc., No. 50, 1976, pp. 72-81.

[97]SS 573.

[98]SS 586.

[99]SS 472.

[100]SS 478. It is important to point out that nowhere does de Beauvoir say motherhood is a natural desire of women. Women desire children for social reasons as opposed to any natural or innate desire. She presupposes what Elizabeth Badinter tries to prove in her recent book, Mother Love: Myth and Reality (New York: Macmillan, 1980).

[101]SS 561.

[102]SS 568.

[103]SS 71.

[104]SS 582.

[105]Friedrich Nietzsche, Thus Spoke Zarathustra, in The Portable Nietzsche, tr. Walter Kaufmann (New York: Viking, 1968), p. 181.

[106]SS 582-586.

[107]_SS_ 573.

[108]Alice Schwartzer, "The Radicalization of Simone de Beauvoir," _Ms._, July, 1972, p. 60.

[109]_SS_ 587.

[110]_SS_ 589.

[111]_SS_ 578.

[112]Simone de Beauvoir and Betty Friedan, "Sex, Society, and the Female Dilemma." _Saturday Review_, June 4, 1975, p. 20.

[113]_SS_ 755.

[114]_SS_ 756.

[115]_Ibid._

[116]_SS_ 757.

[117]_Ibid._

[118]_SS_ 756.

[119]_SS_ 801.

[120]_SS_ 777-778.

[121]_SS_ 777.

[122]_SS_ 778.

[123]_SS_ 781.

[124]_Ibid._

[125]_SS_ 772.

[126]<u>SS</u> 779.

[127]<u>SS</u> 61.

[128]<u>SS</u> 123.

[129]<u>SS</u> 756.

[130]<u>SS</u> 805-806.

[131]<u>SS</u> 806.

CHAPTER THREE

WHAT'S WRONG WITH BEING A HOUSEWIFE?

I. Introduction

Throughout the explication of The Second Sex a number of
questions arose concerning the cogency of de Beauvoir's critique
of the life of the traditional housewife/mother and her position
that women should not be allowed to choose such a vocation. In
this chapter I shall examine many of the questions concerning her
position and attempt to show how most can be answered if one is
willing to go beyond what she says in The Second Sex and look at
some of Sartre's ethical writings and de Beauvoir's earlier book
on ethics, The Ethics of Ambiguity.

It might be useful at this point to divide the questions
into two distinct but related categories. First, there are
questions which are practical or social in nature. For example,
one might ask, given her analysis of the life of the typical
housewife, what changes within the institution of marriage might
solve the problems? Second, there are more basic philosophical
questions. For example, one might question de Beauvoir's position
on what it is to be a human being; that is, her ontology. The
one primary question in this category is how, given her ontology
and her existentialist framework, can she justify her own value

system which underlies her critique of being a housewife/mother? Another important question is how can she justify the continued extolling of the typical "masculine virtues" over the traditional "feminine virtues"?

While these questions fall into two different categories, they are also inter-related. Sartre once said in a letter to Francis Jeanson that ethics must be built on ontology.[1] This is nothing new, as clearly the ethical positions of philosophers from Plato and Aristotle to Mill have grown out of their view of what it means to be a human being at the most fundamental level. In this sense our concern will be to see how in particular an existentialist ontology can be used to generate certain ethical values and hence give a foundation to de Beauvoir's ethical position in The Second Sex.

II. Practical Concerns

There seems to be little question that de Beauvoir is correct in accusing a woman who chooses the life of the typical housewife of bad faith. We have seen that a housewife seeks for the most part to identify herself with her possessions.[2] Since a housewife lacks other forms of self-fulfillment and transcendence, this is only natural. The greater the value of the possessions, the greater worth she gives herself. We have also seen that in taking on such a vocation, a woman tends to turn herself into a thing, "an eternal jewel of changeless beauty."

The role also determines what kinds of activities she will spend her time doing. And, because of the repetitive nature of these activities, her daily round is mechanical and machine-like.

We have also seen that de Beauvoir believes that a woman who chooses the vocation of the traditional housewife/mother is choosing a life of alienated labor. There is likewise little controversy over this claim. It was evident in our last chapter that Marx's description of alienated labor clearly applies to the labor of the typical housewife. A housewife is engaged in boring, repetitive, machine-like labor. Because she is dependent upon her husband, her labor is hired by her husband. She is also alienated from other women through the ongoing competition for more and more beautiful objects through which she seeks to define herself.

And finally, and perhaps most importantly, we have seen how the stultified, sexually frustrated housewife tends to take out her revenge on her children. And beyond actively harming the child, such a woman is a poor role-model for her children. By choosing the role of a housewife and setting such an example, de Beauvoir claims that a woman is implicitly saying to her children (and the rest of the world) that choosing to live the life of the traditional housewife/mother is an acceptable thing for women to do regardless of the oppression involved. As Sartre says in his essay "Existentialism is a Humanism," "When we say that man chooses himself...we mean that in choosing for himself he chooses for

all men."[3] The person is "choosing an image of man such as he
believes he ought to be. To choose between this or that is at
the same time to affirm the value of that which is chosen...I am
creating a certain image of man as I would have him to be."[4] The
question is, given de Beauvoir's analysis which showed all of
the problems that choosing such a role causes, not only for the
person who chooses the role but for women in general, is it
ethical for any woman to make that choice? De Beauvoir's answer
is clearly no. The children who view a mother who has made this
choice will naturally grow up believing that this is an acceptable
life for a woman. They will all believe that it is natural for
women to lead boring, alienated lives. Hence while some might
argue that it is a woman's own business whether or not she chooses
not to work and be a traditional housewife, that it harms no one
but herself, it is de Beauvoir's position that her choice has an
effect upon the beliefs and values of other persons--primarily
her children. It is perpetuating an institution and a supportive
attitude which have been the prime factors in enslaving women as
a class. And if women want to escape this slavery, they must quit
making choices which perpetuate the system.

Unlike many other feminists, de Beauvoir's solution to the
problem is not for women to get paid for their housework and for
housework to be valued more by the society. As we have seen, her
solution is for the society to be changed so that the vocation of
being a "housewife" is no longer a possibility. If housework is

alienated labor and involves a woman in bad faith, it will still
be alienated labor regardless of whether or not she gets paid.
Being paid might even make the problem worse, as wage labor
emphasizes the fact that one's life has been purchased, like the
prostitute's. Secondly, to receive pay for one's work reemphasizes
the fact that a housewife is dependent upon her husband, who is now
openly her employer. One could also imagine the effect of such a
practice on other housewives. Rather than each competing to show
off her possessions, each would compete for higher wages. The
rift between them as human beings would be increased. And finally,
if housework is alienated labor, regardless of whether or not one
receives a wage for it, to be paid would simply make the appeal
of being a housewife even greater. The effect, if de Beauvoir's
analysis is correct, would be to enslave women even more.

Ironically, there is a movement in today's society, due to
there being more and more women professionals, towards house-
husbands. This is supposed to show that doing housework is a
respectable occupation. But given de Beauvoir's critique, housework is boring, stultifying, alienating labor, regardless of
whether it is performed by women or men. Because of this it should
be avoided by both. It degrades the humanity of either sex.

Some, though, might object that with modern technology,
housework is not as bad as de Beauvoir describes. In fact if one
is organized, the duties of washing, cooking, cleaning, etc., can
be done in a relatively short period of time. This allows a

housewife to have a good deal of leisure, and during this leisure,
she could develop her higher potentials as a human being. A
housewife could engage in studying philosophy, writing novels,
or becoming a political activist.

If the point that a woman would still be financially dependent upon her husband is not raised, such a criticism of de
Beauvoir's position is very interesting. However, de Beauvoir
points out that all of a woman's training from childhood on has
equipped her for the function of being a housewife/mother, and,
as long as she can maintain her beauty, being a sex object.
Lacking the proper foundation in education and the corresponding
critical and rational abilities, a housewife, no matter how much
leisure she has, is not equipped to engage in such self-transcendent
activities.

However, in the case of house-husbands, the situation might
be very different. A man who has been trained and has the proper
job experience, might find that the leisure afforded by housework
makes being a house-husband a very inviting role. (I once knew
an English professor who switched roles with his wife and stayed
home. He claimed it was the most productive year of his life.
His household duties took but a few hours, and he spent the
remainder of the day doing research and writing a book.)

Yet, no matter how appealing this may sound, one difference
between a man and a woman who have both taken on the role of the
housekeeper is that the man knows that he is not trapped in that

role. Because of his other abilities, he can give up that "job"
and go into the society to make his own living. The typical
woman, lacking other skills, is condemned to that role for her
life. For a woman, to be a housewife is to choose a vocation; for
a man, it means to choose a job which can at will be changed.
Hence the choice is fundamentally different for each sex.

For all of these reasons, de Beauvoir's position that no
woman should choose to be a housewife appears to be quite defen-
sible. In making such a choice, a woman is choosing a vocation
which is not only mentally stultifying, but will assure her that
she will be economically dependent upon her husband. She is
giving up her freedom much as a person who chooses to be a slave
would be giving up his or her freedom. And, as we have seen,
when a woman makes such a choice, the effects are not simply
self-regarding; she is in effect harming others by perpetuating
an institution which is, according to de Beauvoir's analysis, the
primary cause of the continued oppression of women. In essence,
if women are as a class to become equal to men, the majority of
them cannot continue to choose a vocation which ensures continued
bondage and dependency on men. If true freedom comes only from
economic power and meaningful labor, women must cease choosing
roles which ensure economic dependency.

III. Philosophical Problems

A. The Problem with Values in an Existential Ontology

De Beauvoir's position is clear, and the observations concerning the typical life of the housewife appear to be generally
correct, but there are some important philosophical questions in
terms of ontology and values that need to be asked. First,
concerning her claim that housewives are involved in bad faith,
one might ask, given her ontology, if it is not the case that such
a tendency is present in all human activities, whether these
activities involve housework or leading nations? And if this is
the case, what makes housework different from or any worse than
other forms of bad faith? Or in terms of alienated labor, if all
persons in a capitalist society are involved in alienated labor,
why is housework any worse than being a school teacher? Clearly
some additional standard for judgment must be employed if we are
to claim that a woman's role as a housewife is worse than other
roles.

First, let us see if it is the case that de Beauvoir's
ontology entails that all humans are involved in bad faith. Bad
faith is defined as fleeing from one's freedom in an attempt to
define oneself as a "thing." Her entire analysis of the
male-female relationship has turned on such a view; human beings
flee from their own emptiness and seek to define themselves
through things or other people. For example, in de Beauvoir's

discussion of erotic love we saw that a man and a woman both seek
to find themselves through the other by seducing or oppressing
the other. Apart from that, in her critique of Freud's psycho-
analytic theories, she says that there is a "tendency of the
subject toward alienation. The anxiety that his liberty induces
in the subject leads him to search for himself in things, which is
a kind of flight from himself."[5] Likewise, in her analysis of the
childhood experiences of girls and boys, she says that each child

> ...lives directly the basic drama of every existent:
> that of his relation to the other. Man exper-
> iences with anguish his being turned loose, his
> forlornness. In his flight from freedom, his
> subjectivity, he would fain lose himself in the
> bosom of the Whole...He never succeeds in abolishing
> his separate ego, but at least he wants to attain
> the solidity of the in-himself, the en-soi, to be
> petrified as a thing.[6]

Hence, it does not appear to be unfair to de Beauvoir to
claim that for her bad faith is naturally part of the human
condition. As Richard Bernstein puts it, in his Praxis and Action,
"The existential condition of life is itself bad faith, for in
being condemned to freedom we are also condemned to the impossible
task of trying to identify ourselves with the possibilities we
have chosen, of seeking to become the in-itself-for-itself."[7]
Yet again, if this is the case, why is the bad faith of a housewife
any worse than the bad faith of a male worker or business man or
anyone else for that matter? If bad faith is going to be used as
a standard for criticizing the behavior of the housewife, and if

there are no qualifications in terms of degrees of bad faith,
de Beauvoir has no grounds to judge a housewife's tendencies
towards or involvement in bad faith to be worse than anyone else's.
Yet it is clearly the case that she does pass such a judgment.
Hence in order to be consistent, de Beauvoir must believe that
there are degrees of bad faith and that some activities are
clearly to be preferred to others. And if they are preferred,
they must be preferred because of other values over and above a
person's attempt to take on the identity of a thing. Because all
persons are ontologically structured to always be in bad faith,
some other standard must be found to justify her judgments. The
same argument will apply to using alienated labor as a standard.
If all workers in a capitalist economy are alienated, why is
housework any worse than "putting lug nuts on a Vega"?

But the problem with seeking other values beyond bad faith
and alienation is that de Beauvoir's ontology, which she claims
is based on Sartre's philosophy in Being and Nothingness,[8] appears
to preclude the possibility of grounding other values. That is,
according to the Sartrean existential tradition, all values are
grounded wholly on human choice. As each person might choose
different projects and each choice might result in different
values, the Sartrean position appears to entail a kind of
relativism where one choice is as good as the next, especially if
one freely makes the choice knowing that the value chosen has no
foundation beyond a person's choosing it. As Sartre says, "My

freedom is the unique foundation of values and...<u>nothing</u>,
absolutely nothing, justifies me in adopting this over that particular value, or this or that particular scale of values."[9]   For
Sartre, our individual values are a result of our choices in
terms of our fundamental projects. Once we have chosen a project
as a value, other values become instrumental in the attainment of
our chosen goals.[10] But the nature of the original goal or
project is purely up to the person's free choice. There are no
<u>a priori</u> standards. For a person to posit that one project is
intrinsically more valuable than another is to succumb to what
Sartre calls the "spirit of seriousness" which holds that there are
values quite apart from and "independent of human subjectivity."[11]
In the end, if one adopts this interpretation of Sartre..."it
amounts to the same thing whether one gets drunk alone or is a
leader of nations."[12] The conclusion of such a position is given
by Mary Warnock when she says in her <u>Existential Ethics</u>, "We are
debarred, on pain of bad faith, from asserting that anything is
absolutely valuable."[13] If nothing is absolutely valuable, we
are left with a kind of relativism. Each individual might choose
radically different values as there is no <u>a priori</u> guide to human
choice.

One can certainly support such an interpretation of de
Beauvoir by looking at some of the things she says about ethics
(even though I believe that such an interpretation is wrong). In
the introduction to <u>The Second Sex</u> she tells us that her perspective

is that of "existentialist ethics."[14] She goes on to claim that
all perspectives involve a certain amount of "bias" or "presuppose a relativity of interests"; in fact, "all characteristics
imply values and every description, so called, implies an ethical
background."[15] But the background itself is a "bias."

However, as Socrates says in the Gorgias, a person may say
he or she believes something, but given some of the person's
other claims and actions, it is obvious that in fact the person
does not really hold this position. I believe this is particularly true of de Beauvoir. If one accepts the relativistic
position where all values are merely a matter of personal choice,
then all choices are equally valuable. Yet, as we have seen,
there is ample evidence to believe that de Beauvoir does not
believe that is the case. Throughout The Second Sex it is clear
that she believes that women ought not to choose to be housewives
or sex objects, that there is something very wrong with choosing
either role. She clearly believes that it would be better if
they made other choices. If something is better than something
else, it is better by virtue of an appeal to a higher standard.
And if the standard is to be applied to all women, it must have
some justification beyond de Beauvoir's "bias." (I imagine that
if one were to ask de Beauvoir why she believed it was wrong for
a woman to choose to be a housewife, she would not simply answer,
"Oh, that's simply one of my personal biases." She would un-
doubtedly go on and on giving reasons for her position.)

If, as a result of these difficulties, one refuses to accept
that de Beauvoir is a relativist, one possible solution would be
to look at the actual values that she employs throughout the work
and try to determine if there is some implicit ethical system at
work. After this has been done, the question of justification must
be asked again. That is, given that she does employ other
standards of judgment beyond bad faith and alienation, can these
standards be justified or are they merely values she has chosen
because of her personal "bias"?

One is stuck upon reading The Second Sex with how close many
of the things de Beauvoir says are to the naturalistic tradition
as exemplified in the writings of Aristotle and John Stuart Mill.
There is a tremendous amount of evidence that she may well be
a "closet Aristotlean" in existential guise. Let us examine
these similarities, not only in order to point out her "Aristotelean values," but to see whether these values can be given a
kind of naturalistic justification from within de Beauvoir's
ontology.

As I understand this naturalistic tradition which has its
roots in Aristotle's thought, in order to derive certain values,
one needs to study human behavior and note that human beings
tend to have certain natural desires and certain capacities. For
example, humans naturally desire food, shelter, and sex, and they
have the capacity (practical wisdom) to find the means for
satisfying these desires.[16] One may also observe, like Aristotle,

that "all men by nature desire to know,"[17] and that they have the
capacity for such understanding (contemplative reason). What is
valuable then is the satisfaction of these natural desires, and
the supreme happiness is the active life of satisfying the higher
desires, rather than the mere animal desires for food, sex, and
sensual pleasure.[18] What is immoral is to deny individuals such
self-fulfillment.

This is also Mill's position in his _Utilitarianism_ where he
argues that living a life of satisfying only the animal pleasures
does not lead to happiness.

> The comparison of the Epicurean life to that of
> beasts is felt as degrading, precisely because a
> beast's pleasures do not satisfy a human being's
> conceptions of happiness. Human beings have
> faculties more elevated than the animal appetites,
> and, when once made conscious of them, do not
> regard anything as happiness which does not
> include their gratification...It is better to be
> a human being dissatisfied than a pig satisfied.[19]

Likewise in _The Subjection of Women_, Mill argues that happiness
is having an outlet for our higher human faculties. "There is
nothing, after disease, indigence, and guilt so fatal to the
pleasurable enjoyment of life as the want of a worthy outlet of
our active faculties."[20] Hence, according to Mill, because
women are often denied such an active outlet for their truly
human faculties they are not happy.

Mill's emphasis on the importance of human liberty is also
very close to de Beauvoir's position. For Mill, humans have

natural capacities and the desire to realize these capacities, thus they desire the freedom to do so; "...freedom is the first and strongest want of human nature."[21] In On Liberty, he argues that individual liberty must be unrestrained as long as the liberty does not harm others.[22]

In summary, this naturalistic approach holds that a human being's function is to realize his or her capacities to the fullest extent, and that institutions, dogmas, or groups of people that stand in the way of such self-realization are evil and to be opposed.

One can cite numerous passages to show that de Beauvoir holds this kind of naturalistic approach to values and shares a good deal with both Aristotle (the essentialist) and Mill. In the Introduction to The Second Sex she states that "For our part, we hold that the only public good is that which assures the private good of the citizens; we shall pass judgment on institutions according to their effectiveness in giving concrete opportunities to individuals."[23] "Concrete opportunities" are defined as the liberty or freedom to engage in projects "that serve as a mode of transcendence" and allow the individual to achieve liberty "through a continual reaching out toward other liberties."[24] What she opposes is "stagnation" or the "degradation of existence into the 'en-soi' -- the brutish life of subjection to given conditions."[25] If the person allows himself or herself to be subjected to such a "brutish life," "this downfall represents a moral fault,...If it is inflicted upon him, it spells frustration and oppression. In both cases it is an <u>absolute</u> <u>evil</u>."[26] With such a clear statement of ethical values, which concludes that some acts are "absolute evil," one can certainly question whether de Beauvoir is a relativist. Her position is rather like Aristotle's; given human nature, whatever stands in the way of natural development of human capacities is evil.

We have already seen that throughout <u>The Second Sex</u>, de Beauvoir extols the virtues of creative labor and the active life as opposed to the passive life of the typical female. This position also mirrors Aristotle's values in his <u>Nichomachean</u> <u>Ethics</u>. Her notion of self-realization through transcendent labor is analogous to his idea that one becomes what one becomes by engaging in meaningful labor or creation. To <u>do</u> nothing is to <u>be</u> nothing. As Aristotle says in his analysis of artistic creation "what he is in potential, his handiwork manifests in activity."[27] As we have seen, de Beauvoir's criticism of housework turns on just such an analysis of self-realization. A housewife's activity is meaningless repetition, hence her higher human potentials are never realized. (Of course de Beauvoir believes, unlike Aristotle, that these potentials are present in women.) Secondly, Aristotle's notion of the truly happy life, as well as pleasure, always emphasizes the active over the passive. He argues that activity must be a part of the happy life; other- wise we would have to count the virtuous man who is asleep in a

coma as happy.[28] Likewise his analysis of pleasure sees it as
the result of "the best activity...of the best-conditioned organ
in relation to the finest of its objects."[29] In the same sense
the value of the active life over the passive is given in his
description of happiness as contemplation, which emphasizes this
notion of a human's highest faculty, theoretical reason, actively
thinking about the highest of objects, "God."[30]

This emphasis on the active as opposed to the passive underlies all of de Beauvoir's criticisms of the life of a young
female child and her criticism of the life of a housewife. The
life of the little girl is repeatedly criticized for the girl's
being led to choose the passive role of a sex-object, as opposed
to the more active role of the young boy who is encouraged to
investigate the world and in so doing, develops his rational
capacities.[31] According to de Beauvoir, denying the young girl
an active life and effective outlets for her natural desires
plays an important part in the girl's becoming the resentful
woman she typically becomes.

Another striking similarity between Aristotle and de
Beauvoir is their analyses of leisure. Of all whom de Beauvoir
has criticized, women of the upper class, "the leisured women,"
are the most vehemently attacked. Even though such women may
consider themselves happy because of their leisure, it is clear
for de Beauvoir that such happiness is not the purpose of life.[32]
Because they do nothing to realize their higher capacities or to

156

make a better world, she calls them "the most useless nonentities ever produced by the human species.[33] In the same sense, Aristotle too holds that leisure and amusement are not the purpose of living; rather one engages in leisure so that one may have the needed energies to engage in meaningful labor. "Relaxation... is taken for the sake of activity."[34] Hence, from this perspective, to choose to be the leisurely upper-class housewife would be to deny one's true happiness. It would be to mistake a means for an end. It would be to confuse the true happiness that comes from meaningful activities with the quietude of stagnation. It would be to confuse Mill's "pig pleasures" with human pleasures.

Even though de Beauvoir is openly critical of Aristotle for his view of women, for his essentialist view of nature, and for his notion of virtue as the "Golden Mean," (she refers to it as the morality of mediocrity),[35] her way of understanding human development and happiness appears ironically to be very close to the naturalist tradition grounded in Aristotle's thought.

There is one final point of similarity which may cause some readers of de Beauvoir to question the fairness of her description of women; that is, her own values are those typically labeled as "masculine." (In fact, many of my students have accused her of being a female intellectual who was bitter because she was not a man.) When she lists traits that she considers desirable for all human beings to possess, the traits are always

the traditional "masculine virtues," much like the picture of
the ideal man which could be taken from Aristotle's Nichomachean
Ethics.

Aristotle's ideal man is one who possesses the Greek moral
virtues of courage, self-control, rational understanding, and a
continual desire for knowledge of all kinds; he is straightforward, has an adequate self concept such that he takes pride
in himself and his self-development; he desires honor, but being
honorable, he will not compromise himself; he is not concerned
with trifling matters and is above pettiness; he is charitable,
but only to the extent that will truly benefit those who receive;
he will risk his life for high ideals, as he "knows there are
conditions on which life is not worth having"; he is independent,
and prefers to benefit rather than being benefitted; his concern
should be above the small things of everyday life, while he aims
at higher things; he must also be "open in his hate," secret
revenge or coquetting are beneath him; he is independent of
others, and refuses to live vicariously; he refuses to carry a
grudge when wronged; he will not gossip; even his gait and voice
are even and never excited, and finally he is disdainful of
those who adorn themselves with fancy clothing.[36]

Given our explication of de Beauvoir's criticisms of
feminine behavior, Aristotle's description of the ideal appears as
if it were the standard that she uses to condemn the behavior of
most women. All behavior which is typically called "feminine"

falls outside of this model. According to de Beauvoir, because
of the way women are raised and treated in society, they do in
fact lack rationality; rather than being self-controlled they are
easily excited and emotional;[37] any desire for knowledge that
they have is of the most mundane sort; they lack courage, for
they have never been taught to stand up for their rights; rather
than being straightforward, women are crafty and coquettish;
their pride is not in their own transcendence or in developing
their real abilities, but rather in their appearance, which is
typically cosmetic rather than real; rather than being independent,
women are totally dependent on the men who support them; rather
than being open with their hate, they are vengeful and secretive;
and women's propensity toward gossip and idle talk hardly need
be mentioned. De Beauvoir's description of women is the antithesis of Aristotle's description of the "ideal man." And
basically, what she urges women to become is like the Aristotelean
ideal. She has complained that to be a woman contradicts being
human.[38] And, for her, "being human" in the fullest sense means
being as much like Aristotle's ideal as possible.

From such evidence, a case can be made that de Beauvoir's
values are based on this Aristotelean tradition and that far from
being a relativist, she believes that the development of certain
human capacities such as reason, understanding, and logic[39] are
clearly superior to others because these capacities are those which
are special for the human species. This is why she argues that

having babies is not a truly "human" function, as biological reproduction is proper to all animals.[40] While the first question as to the nature of her values has been answered, the second question, concerning the justification of these values is not easily answered.

According to thinkers in the naturalist tradition, those things or qualities are valuable which are naturally desired or are means to fulfilling natural desires. According to Aristotle, humans have the desires they have because of their essential nature peculiar to the human species. Hence, Aristotle can begin his Metaphysics with the statement, "All men by nature desire to know."[41] Because de Beauvoir in her chapter on the biological explanation of feminine behavior has specifically argued against the essentialist tradition, she cannot give the Aristotelean account of the origin of certain desires. This would be to adopt values prior to human choice.

However, she could be employing the Sartrean notion of a shared "human condition" which is similar in effect to Aristotle's notion. That is to say, that if humans share a "human condition" in terms of their environment and ontological structure, then they will have similar needs. These needs (food, shelter, sex, etc.) will generate desires, and these desires in turn will generate human values. Such reasoning is close to Mill's "proof" that human happiness is the end for which all humans aim. As he says in his Utilitarianism, "the sole evidence...that anything is desirable is that people desire it."[42] Desire becomes the ground of morality while the ground of desire, at least at the most basic level, is need. And needs are for the most part universal due to the human condition. Such an analysis is echoed by Sartre in his Critique of Dialectical Reason, in his discussion of need as the source of values. There he says that "need...is in fact the revelation of a goal to aim at."[43] And our values are what we choose as goals and the means to attaining our goals.

The problem is that while such an analysis of values in terms of desires and needs may be able to serve as some sort of a moral standard at a very general level, how can this alone serve as a standard by which one can judge levels of bad faith or which role is superior to another? It would seem that any role would have value in so far as that role aided the person or was a means to the person's satisfying his or her basic needs. Hence if a particular woman chose to be a housewife in order to satisfy her needs for security, food, shelter, and sex, then this role would have to be allowed in so far as it did satisfy these needs. Even if it can be shown that adopting this role has the tendency to result in not satisfying the needs of the class of women as a whole, it would still not follow that choosing the role would be wrong for the individual. It may not be the pru- dential thing for the woman to do, given all of the problems with being a housewife, but if the only criterion for valuing anything is the satisfaction of individual human needs then the role of the housewife cannot be eliminated.

Yet de Beauvoir might answer this objection by saying that no woman ought to choose to be a housewife as a means to satisfying her basic desires because "as a general rule" the woman's truly human desires--those for creativity, self-realization, and meaningful human relations--will be stultified. But, conversely, it is very difficult to be creative when one is hungry or poverty stricken. Choosing to be a housewife may be the surest way out of poverty. Be that as it may, there do seem to be very large numbers of human beings who do not particularly desire de Beauvoir's values of creativity, rational understanding, or human relations beyond "idle talk" with one's neighbor. And this is the crucial point: once one moves beyond the basic animal needs, the nature and extent of human desires does not seem to fit any a priori model. Many human beings appear perfectly content to spend most of their time watching television. Others are not.

Such a phenomenon is a real problem for anyone who tries to base a value system on human desires. It is relatively easy at the animal level to base values on the desires to satisfy human biological needs. These needs are relatively identical in the human species. But beyond these basic needs, human desires vary to a large extent. If, as Mill said, we know that something is desirable because it is desired, then anything that is desired will be desirable. Hence, if some woman desires to be a housewife,

162

or slave for that matter, then by definition being a housewife has
value and is to be allowed. Anything at all becomes acceptable
behavior as long as humans desire it. Or conversely, if people
did not desire some state of affairs then that state of affairs
would be devoid of value.[44] An interesting example of this lack
of desire, according to de Beauvoir and Sartre, is the case of
freedom. Sartre has pointed out that we are condemned to be
free and that we naturally are disposed through bad faith to try
to escape that condition, to deny our freedom. If desire were
the ultimate ground of values then freedom would have no value for
those who desire security. Yet in "Existentialism is a Humanism,"
Sartre argues that the quest for freedom should be man's ultimate
goal.[45] Likewise, de Beauvoir says in The Ethics of Ambiguity,
"The man who seeks to justify his life must want freedom itself
absolutely and above all else."[46] But in fact, many or most do
not desire freedom. Hence, desire cannot be the ultimate ground
of values for de Beauvoir. If it is, bad faith is a value, because
many desire it.

It is de Beauvoir's emphasis on the universal importance of
freedom and her analysis of bad faith as naturally desired that
make the attempt to ground values on human desires untenable. On
one hand, de Beauvoir extols the values which have grown out of
the naturalistic position, but cannot adopt any justification for
the position which tries to ground values on desires or disposition. We must look elsewhere for a justification.

One possible solution to the problem of justifying her naturalistic values lies in a reinterpretation of her project, that is, that de Beauvoir's philosophical method, as a phenomenological description of woman's situation, does not need to provide a logical justification of her ultimate ethical values. Like Mill and Aristotle, de Beauvoir may hold that a justification of ultimate values is logically impossible. As Mill says in his Utilitarianism, "Questions of ultimate ends are not subject to direct proof. Whatever can be proved to be good must be so by being shown to be a means to something admitted to be good without proof...to be incapable of proof by reasoning is common to all first principles."[47] Likewise, Aristotle points out in his Posterior Analytics that first principles cannot be derived deductively from higher order principles; otherwise the truth of the first principles would be dependent upon one's acceptance of even higher first principles, and so on ad infinitum.[48] Aristotle proposes that upon a careful examination of the subject matter, the active intellect (nous) just sees the nature of the first principle in question. De Beauvoir's use of the phenomenological method as a careful description of woman's situation may be an attempt, in some sense like Aristotle's, to show the reader what it is like to be a woman. The reader is then supposed to just see that, given the description, there are clearly oppressive forces at work which destroy or supremely limit the woman's autonomy. The description, like a good poem, discloses

the truth of the situation to the reader in such a clear and
convincing manner that the reader will just see that the description and the values employed are correct. The woman who reads
The Second Sex might say "Yes, that's how it is to be a young girl,
housewife, mother, or working woman." If she consents to the
description, she at the same time consents to the values objecti-
fied in the description.

That de Beauvoir and Sartre were impressed by the prospects
offered by phenomenological description as a philosophical method
is evident. Wilfred Desan, in his book The Marxism of Jean-Paul
Sartre, tells of Sartre's excitement when he heard of Husserl's
method, "philosophy was no longer to consist of an inquiry into
origin or of a deductive exploration for invisible substances
and causes; philosophy was to be a description of that which
appears insofar as it appears, a disclosure of the concrete, a
revelation of all that falls under our senses, whether inside
or outside ourselves."[49] De Beauvoir echoes this same enthusiasm
towards using the approach of phenomenological description.

"There are two ways of seizing and explaining metaphysical
reality. One can attempt to elucidate the universal significance
in an abstract language. In this case theory takes a universal
and timeless form. Or one can incorporate into the doctrine the
concrete and dramatic aspect of experience and propose not some
sort of abstract truth, but my truth, as I realize it in my own

life. This is the existentialist way...The purpose is to grasp existence in the act itself, in which it fulfills itself."[50]

The Second Sex can easily be seen as this sort of subjective approach which arrives at some sort of universal truth about the condition of women, not through a rigorous chain of arguments, but through a careful description from de Beauvoir's point of view of what it is like to be and live as a woman. And, although the point of view is de Beauvoir's, she clearly believes that it is a privileged point of view which has universal application to the class of women as a whole. She believes that she is describing "the phenomena of everyday life as they are lived."[51]

If one disagrees with de Beauvoir's description, she would say that is simply because one's consciousness has not been raised, that one still perceives the world of women through the mystifications perpetuated by our Western culture; i.e., that the feminine essence is eternal, that women are naturally irrational, or that marriage is a woman's natural path to happiness. In this sense, one could see The Second Sex as an attempt to describe in concrete terms the situation of modern women so that the reader with a minimally developed ethical sense can plainly see the many injustices hidden by the traditional mystification of women.

Unfortunately, if this is de Beauvoir's approach to the problem of justifying her values there are a number of problems. It seems that such a phenomenological approach has a striking similarity to the intuitionist tradition in ethics. Both intimately rely on a kind of "direct seeing" by the reader to justify their conclusions. The major problem is to explain the variance in "what is directly seen" by different people. Of course, one can argue that the differences in agreement can be explained in terms of prejudice, mystification, or general lack of insight. De Beauvoir also says that some women fail to perceive the truth of their oppressed state because they perceive it to be in their own best interest to support the existing state of affairs.[52] This is especially true of bourgeois housewives. This is the same argument given by Marxists to explain why many workers in capitalist societies fail to see that they are being exploited. Such workers falsely believe the system is fair because they believe capitalism benefits them more than the alternatives.

The failure to see the oppressive structures of a social situation is a function of one's willingness to accept or criticize the framework of traditional society. Ideally, if all were equally enlightened, all would perceive the truth of de Beauvoir's values. One would just see that it is better to be active than passive, that it is better to be rational rather than emotional, that it is better to be free rather than dependent.

Such an interpretation of de Beauvoir's approach to the problem of values and their justification is given further credence when one looks at Sartre's discussion of the "human condition" as

being universal. His talk of a shared human condition would mean
that, even though we are not all alike due to some a priori
essence, we all share problems common to being human.[53] If there
is a truth about human beings as a class, and if there are also
certain ontological similarities that constitute human reality,
then the possibility of all human beings recognizing certain
truths and agreeing to their relevance is supremely enhanced. On
the other hand, if each person is radically different in structure
and in terms of the human condition, then the world will appear
radically different to each. The possibility of a phenomenological
description having universal appeal turns on the shared characteristics of the persons who read the description.[54]

However, even if we add Sartre's notion of a "human
condition" to the notion of a phenomenological description dis-
closing some universal characteristics about the lived experience
of the typical woman, I believe that there are still problems.
The first problem may be seen by some as minor, but on the other
hand some philosophers in the analytic tradition would certainly
bring it up. Someone like Karl Popper would surely want to
question de Beauvoir concerning the falsifiability of parts of
her description.[55]

There are some radical claims in The Second Sex. De
Beauvoir claims that marriage is "obscene in principle," "generally
not founded upon love," or a "life that slips away gently toward
death without questioning its purpose."[56] Someone like Popper

might say that he does not "see" the truth of these statements.
De Beauvoir's rejoinder might be that Popper's paternalistic
point of view had so biased his perspective that he could no
longer see the truth. From Popper's perspective, the problem
with such a response is that it appears that absolutely nothing
is allowed to falsify de Beauvoir's claims. Any objection to her
claim is seen merely as a sign of the objector's biases and a
sign of unlightened point of view due to social conditioning.
Popper's position is that if an assertion cannot be falsified then
it is void of any scientific content. While the assertion may have
some meaning in terms of emotion, it is not one whose truth or
falsity can be known scientifically.

Someone like Popper might argue that he sees the life of
the married-housewife-mother as a noble, fulfilling existence
where the woman, 'bless her heart,' works at making a pleasant
environment for her husband who works hard all day at the
philosophy department, takes care of their wonderful children in
a way no day-care center could, has plenty of leisure to develop
her mental capacities, and has close human relationships with all
of the other faculty wives. He would ask de Beauvoir why his
description was any less correct than hers. If the truth of
the description comes down to some sort of "intuitive seeing,"
then the description cannot be disproved by any alternative
"seeing," that is to say, it is unfalsifiable, and hence

meaningless. (I think it would be interesting to hear how de Beauvoir might deal with such a criticism.)

Another problem with trying to ground her value claims on a phenomenological description is that although it may be the case that if one accepts such a thing as the "human condition" and some version of the Sartrean ontology of human existence, one can see that certain fundamental values are implied, yet other more particular values may not be so clearly seen. As we saw in the criticism of the naturalistic attempt to ground values on a human condition and human desire, there is a problem with ever going beyond fundamental human needs if one is attempting to ground all values. It may be the case that all human beings can "see" that food, shelter, and sex are values, and can hence see how any set of social conditions or institutions which destroy these values ought to be opposed, but beyond these, it is not obvious why for example all of those typically "masculine" values that de Beauvoir extols should be adopted universally. We have already seen that many people do not in fact question "feminine" values. If we hold that these people are merely unenlightened, we are back to the problem of falsifiability.

What needs to be given is an account of the ontological structure of human beings, coupled with an account of the human condition such that the acceptance of certain fundamental values entails the acceptance of other values. The notion of entailment here means showing how the attainment of the fundamental values is possible only if certain other values are upheld by the society or the individual. Although de Beauvoir does not offer such an account, I believe that one can be given. The importance of such an account is paramount because only then will we be able to see clearly why some forms of bad faith are preferable to others, why women ought not to choose to be sex objects, why the life of a housewife ought not be allowed, and why one form of alienated labor is better than another. In short, what is at stake here is nothing less than rational justification for her entire project in The Second Sex. Otherwise, her description may be nothing more than her prejudices. (Although, given how closely her values resemble Aristotle's and Mill's, one might say that her prejudices show a certain amount of "philosophical good taste." One could certainly do worse.)

Let us return to de Beauvoir's ontology. She has claimed that her ethics is based on Sartre's ontology. What needs to be done is to show how her ontology entails certain fundamental values and how the acquisition of these values entails other related values, such as those which she shares with the Aristotelean tradition.

B. Towards Justifying de Beauvoir's Value System

It appears that we have reached an impasse in the attempt to justify de Beauvoir's rather naturalistic values in terms of either natural desire or an intuitive seeing of the values in the phenomenological perspective. We have seen what her values are and that her fundamental value is human freedom, and that she is opposed to any institution which limits human freedom.[57] But there does not appear to be an argument in The Second Sex to justify ultimately the value of freedom and the other Aristotelean values which she extols women to seek.

As I have already said, I agree with Sartre that ethics must be grounded on ontology; that is, what one perceives as the fundamental nature of human beings will determine to a large extent what values one prescribes in one's moral philosophy. As Sartre says, "ontology cannot be separated from ethics."[58] What needs to be done is first to show how the Sartrean ontology to which de Beauvoir subscribes entails that freedom is the fundamental value, and secondly how there is a logical relationship between the value of freedom and the other values that she holds, such that if one values human freedom, one is committed to valuing the other values such as creativity, critical thought, rational understanding of the world, and self-control.

One further problem which must be confronted is that of being able to universalize these values. Even if they can be established for individuals, de Beauvoir's position in The Second Sex is not only arguing that each woman should seek freedom, truth, and self-realization because that will bring her happiness; she is arguing that women should organize and actively seek these values for all women. Showing that each individual needs to pursue his or her individual freedom is very different from showing that one needs to seek freedom for all. In other words, if it can be shown that humans ought to seek freedom, it is not intuitively 'clear' why each individual who values his own freedom should seek the freedom of all. Or, in the case of women, even if it can be shown that a woman should not choose to be married and a housewife/mother, it is not clear why a woman should try to get other women to oppose these vocations. In fact, a woman might see that the more women who remain in the traditional roles, as housewives, the better her chances for a good job outside of that role.

1.) Two Senses of Freedom

We have seen from what de Beauvoir says in the introduction to The Second Sex that she is absolutely opposed to any institution which destroys or, without justification, limits human liberty or freedom.[59] Before we attempt to show why freedom is the fundamental value for her, it is extremely important to distinguish between two uses of the word "freedom" in both Sartre's and de Beauvoir's thinking. If this distinction is not made many confusions will result.

One sense of the notion of freedom is grounded in the ontological nature of human beings. As we have seen, both Sartre and de Beauvoir believe that in so far as a human being is essentially consciousness, a human is essentially nothing but freedom. Because of this, humans cannot take on the identity of a thing. This freedom is not a quality tacked on to a person like being tall or female; this sense of freedom is the very being of human beings.

When Sartre divides the world into two categories, the "in-itself" and the "for-itself" (things and consciousness), he argues that consciousness cannot be a mere thing because consciousness is always conscious of things.[60] However, consciousness is not a passive mirror reflecting the outer thing or inner feeling of which it is conscious. (That would be to turn consciousness into a kind of thing.) Rather consciousness is intentional; it is continually choosing and positing objects of consciousness. It must choose from among the myriad of possibilities present at each moment which of the possible objects to posit as an awareness. Because consciousness is free nothing can force it to posit one object over another.

The intentional nature of consciousness, makes possible such negative judgments as "The world is not as it might be." To make such judgments, consciousness must be able to freely withdraw from the world of the in-itself and imagine a different state of affairs. Such negative judgments, according to Sartre, show that consciousness reveals a "nothingness" or lack in the world, while the world "in-itself" is complete.[61] All things (the in-itself) are self-identical; their being does not depend on the being of another, while the being of consciousness as freedom is always to

be conscious of something, even if that something is a lack. Consciousness is, at this fundamental level, a freedom which must
transcend itself towards objects other than itself, and has its
being only through this transcendence. That is to say, consciousness is, as Sartre says, "a being-which-is-not-what-it-is and
which-is-what-it-is-not...."[62]

Because this _freedom_ is the essence of consciousness, it
cannot be destroyed or oppressed this side of death. Hence if
this is the only sense of freedom that de Beauvoir uses, then all
of her talk of certain institutions destroying or even limiting
human freedom is senseless. This ontological freedom cannot be
limited because in any given situation consciousness must always
choose how to posit and interpret the situation. Human beings
can always say 'yes' or 'no.' They can either accept the situation or say no and revolt against it. For Sartre, no situation in
itself can force human beings to consent or act against their
will.[63] Man must choose because consciousness is freedom. Even
to choose not to choose is still to choose; "Man is condemned to
be free."

The second sense of freedom is related to the first. Not
only is consciousness free in terms of its intentionality and
its ability to either affirm or negate the chosen object of
consciousness, but there is also the freedom to shape the situation in such a way that the goals posited by consciousness are
attained. The distinction is made clear when Sartre gives his

account of human action in <u>Being and Nothingness</u>.[64] There he

describes four distinct moments of consciousness which are

involved in human action. The first is the immediate positing of

the situation by consciousness. This positing is the product of

man's immediate ontological freedom. Second, consciousness then

<u>may</u> freely choose to reflect upon its awareness of the situation

such that it perceives the situation as a lack in which something

is missing and could be different. Then, it can either affirm

this lack or negate it. Neither requires or necessarily leads to

action. If a person believes that the situation is the way it

is because of forces beyond his or her power or is so "immersed

in the situation...he cannot imagine that he can exist in it

otherwise,"[65] no <u>action</u> results. The positing of the situation

and the choosing of an attitude towards it are part of conscious-

ness' original freedom which it <u>is</u>. While the nature of the

attitude or one's choice is due to one's awareness of possibilities

present in the situation, <u>that</u> one chooses an attitude is not a

contingent matter. But if the person perceives the lack, begins

to imagine a different state of affairs, and finally acts to

realize the imagined state of affairs, we are now into the realm

of freedom which is different from ontological freedom: the

freedom which is the freedom to act. While a person's ontological

freedom cannot be limited, one's freedom to act can be limited in

a number of ways. One can limit the person's access to education

so that the person cannot imagine any other state of affairs besides

the status quo. Or if the person does develop a kind of revolutionary consciousness, one can limit his or her freedom to act
simply by keeping the person poor, denying the necessary tools
for revolution, or keeping the person so busy trying to earn a
subsistence wage that the person has not the time or energy to
organize any revolutionary activity.

Obviously this aspect of Sartre's analysis can be applied
very easily to the situation of the typical housewife. The housewife may feel in her heart of hearts that something is seriously
missing from her life, but due to lack of education, the mystification of her role as a housewife/mother, and her isolation from
other women, her freedom to posit a goal which would change her
situation and to act on that goal are supremely limited.

The second use of the word "freedom" is the freedom for
consciousness to withdraw from its immersion in the situation,
actively posit new goals, and then act on those goals. This
second notion of freedom is the one of which de Beauvoir is
speaking in the introduction to The Second Sex where she says
she opposes any situation or institution which limits the freedom
of others.[66] The ontological freedom that man is cannot be
limited, but freedom to imagine a better world and act on that
vision can be limited.

2.) A Transcendental Argument for the Value of Human Freedom

If the distinction is reasonably clear, the next step in the argument is to show why freedom in this second sense is the ultimate value. What needs to be kept in mind is that this proof must escape the criticism we have put forward of any attempt to ground ethical values merely on human desire or human choice. Both attempts lead to a relativism which cannot support de Beauvoir's claims. If freedom is the ultimate value, it must be so regardless of whether people desire it or choose it. The proof must show that if anything at all has value, then freedom has.

The proof that can be given is a kind of transcendental argument that is based on Sartre's ontology. Given Sartre's notion of the world as it is, identical with itself, it is obvious to him that values are not to be found in the world as it is in itself. Sartre's position resembles Hume's point in his Treatise on Human Nature where he points out that one has never had an impression of a value. The sense impressions of a man and a good man (in the moral sense of good) are identical. Hence, according to Hume, values are not to be located in the world of sense. In Sartre's language, values are not to be found in the world of the in-itself. Hence human values must be grounded in human consciousness, the for-itself. As he says in Being and Nothingness:

> Value...does not deliver itself to a contemplative
> intuition which would apprehend it as <u>being</u>
> value...On the contrary, it can be revealed only
> to an active freedom which makes it exist as value
> by the sole fact of recognizing it as such...my
> freedom is the unique foundations of values.[68]

If human choice or freedom is the foundation for all values,
then human freedom as a necessary condition for <u>any</u> value whatsoever must itself be the fundamental value. That is to say, <u>if</u>
anything is valuable, human freedom is valuable simply because
nothing can have value apart from freedom giving it value. Another
way to put the argument is, if X is valuable, then any condition
for the very possibility of X is also valuable. For example, if
life is valuable, then the conditions necessary for life, i.e.,
food and shelter, must (in the logical sense) also be valued. Or
as Kant says, one cannot consistently will the <u>end</u> without
willing the <u>means</u>. Human freedom, as the foundation of all values,
must itself be the fundamental value, because without freedom
there is no value.

To apply this argument to Sartre's analysis of action may
be helpful. Human beings, according to Sartre, desire certain
states of affairs to come into existence which presently do not
exist. Thus, they value the envisioned state of affairs. If one
values the envisioned state of affairs, one must, to be consistent,
value the conditions which allowed one to first envision the
state of affairs <u>and</u> the means to realize this state of affairs
in the world. There are two such conditions: Freedom of thought

and freedom of action: the freedom to envision the possible state of affairs and then to act in such a way to bring the possible into reality.

Obviously, not all human desires are merely for those things necessary for mere biological existence. In fact, both Sartre and de Beauvoir believe that human beings desire above all else to give some meaning to their lives. This separates humans from animals.[69] Ultimately, as we saw in our first chapter, this is the desire to be a free, self-conscious being whose existence no longer needs to be justified; in other words, human beings desire to be God. These attempts to be God take on the myriad of behaviors--seeking fame, the life of pleasure, the life of power, making someone fall in love with us, etc. Yet all of these attempts at self-justification depend upon the freedom to choose certain projects and hence give them whatever value they have. As de Beauvoir says in The Ethics of Ambiguity, "Freedom is the source from which all significations and all values spring; it is the original condition of all justification of existence. The man who wants to justify his life must want freedom itself absolutely and above everything else."[70]

The argument as stated is hypothetical. If one values any-thing at all, and if one desires to give one's life any meaning whatsoever, one must value freedom. As Thomas Anderson says in The Foundation and Structure of Sartrean Ethics, "If I do not value

my freedom how can I consistently value any value it creates...
because all values come only from freedom."[71]

Yet because the argument is hypothetical, one might plausi-
bly want to question the truth of one of its antecedents. Why
should we believe that at some fundamental level humans desire
some justification for their lives? It would seem that given
Sartre's and de Beauvoir's position concerning the foundation of
all values, justifying one's life would have value if and only
if human freedom gave it value. This sort of objection is brought
up by Richard Bernstein in his Praxis and Action. There he argues
that any attempt to ground values beyond human choice always contradicts Sartre's ontology. The chasm between the ontological
and the moral is an unbridgeable one."[72] If freedom is the
ultimate foundation of all values, no value except freedom itself
can exist without being freely chosen. Hence, if justifying
one's existence has value, its value must be grounded in human
consciousness freely choosing to give it value.

However, other interpreters of Sartre have pointed out that
one simply needs to make the distinction between those values
which are consciously chosen and "non-reflective values" which
are implied when one understands the ontological nature of consciousness.[73] What Sartre means by claiming that humans seek
some justification for their lives is simply that consciousness
because of its very nature must choose. Each particular choice
is part of consciousness' pre-reflective desire to be. The only

alternative to choosing and hence giving some justification to
one's existence is to choose suicide. Hence, the simple fact
that people continue to live means that they have <u>chosen</u> to
continue to live, and this entails that they are engaged in giving
life meaning.

As I understand this sort of argument, there is a distinction between values which are chosen by consciousness and values
which are logically implied whenever consciousness chooses, and
being condemned to be free, consciousness cannot choose not to
choose. Even though one may not consciously choose to "justify
one's life," the very fact that one continues to live and hence
choose implies that life is justified to that person. Otherwise
the person would commit suicide.

3.) Justifying "Masculine Virtues" in Terms of Freedom:

If we grant that freedom, the freedom to envision the
possible and to act, is the ultimate value for de Beauvoir and
accept the transcendental argument which shows that if anything has
value, freedom does, there are still a number of questions which
need to be discussed. First, we must see if de Beauvoir can give
some justification, based on the standard of freedom, for
criticizing the housewife's role and all of the values that that
entails. Second, we must see if granting freedom as the ultimate
value allows her to justify her rather Aristotelean values, as
opposed to the more nurturing "feminine virtues." And finally

we must see if using individual freedom as a standard can lead
to the conclusion that we ought to be concerned for the freedom
of others; that is, that women ought to be concerned for the
freedom of other women.

We have seen that freedom means to transcend the present
through positing a meaningful project and carrying out that
project through labor. De Beauvoir's description of housework
as repetitive, alienated labor appears to be the antithesis of
such active self-realization. The housewife's daily routine is a
kind of negative labor which aims at fighting the forces of life
in order to maintain the status quo--a clean house, clean clothes,
and the daily round of cooking and washing dishes. There is no
transcendence here; her life is mere immanence. Her human
capacities remain forever mere possibilities, but possibilities
that are seldom even imagined because she sees her role as being
the result of forces beyond her control. To be a housewife is
simply seen as women's plight in the "natural order" of things.
Her role closes off the possibilities that men must have for
self-transcendence.

In the introduction to The Second Sex, de Beauvoir holds
that the liberty which a person possesses is directly proportional
to her possibilities. The housewife's role limits her possibilities, not only for meaningful projects, but by making her
financially dependent upon her husband. (Even if he pays her,
she is still dependent upon him.) Being financially dependent and

lacking the needed skills for success in the world of business,
the options open to anyone who chooses the vocation of a housewife are few.

Another aid to freedom, in the sense of the freedom to act
to achieve one's goals, is a rational understanding of the
world. If one has a problem, the ability to solve the problem
is contingent upon one's ability first to perceive that there
is a problem, to understand its nature and causes, and finally
the ability to alter the causes or nullify the effects. However,
as we have seen, from the time a woman is a young girl, she has
been denied the development of her natural rational faculties.
If, as Aristotle would say, the potentials are never given the
chance to be used, these potentials will never become actual.
By being denied access to the real world, a woman never develops
the rational capacities needed to solve her problems. Hence,
her freedom to act is supremely limited.

If creativity is a part of freedom, a housewife will lack
that too. This is because, according to de Beauvoir,
creativity needs the raw material gathered from experience in
order to fashion a new state of affairs or a work of art. In
being denied access to the world, a housewife lacks the needed
raw material for true creativity.[74]

Because a woman lacks a rational understanding of the underlying causes for events or human behavior, she substitutes
trickery and coquettry for reason. These dishonest behaviors

are enemies of her freedom because these character traits assure
her that she will not be accepted as an equal in the community
of working men where such behavior is looked at as an extreme
enemy of the trust that is usually presupposed in business
relations. Trickery and emotional displays are no substitute
for rational argument.[75]

One might ask if it is not the case that many traditional
male jobs do not also limit human freedom. De Beauvoir admits
that there are such limits on men.[76] But at least men tend to
be trained for employment in a wide variety of places. They are
not limited to being dependent on one person--their spouse. And,
a person can change jobs far more easily than one can change
spouses. And, if a woman is older and has a number of dependent
children, her 'marketability' is supremely diminished.

One might argue that in this age of specialization, men
too are as equally disadvantaged as women, especially if men are
trained in one special area and the demand for workers in that
area decreases. A case in point may be that of the man trained
to be a philosophy professor. What other opportunities are
open to the Ph.D. in philosophy whose area of expertise is
Russell's Theory of Descriptions?

De Beauvoir though would probably argue that although the
male Ph.D. in philosophy may find that getting a job in that
area is difficult, his training in critical thinking and the
accompanying communications skills makes him far more

marketable in the business world than a woman who, because she always thought she would be taken care of by a man, did not take her education seriously.[77] A woman's education and her job experience _qua_ housewife have not equipped her for any marketable skill beyond being a housekeeper. Her possibilities are supremely limited.

All persons are free, but their freedom is always in a determinate situation with a determinate number of possibilities. De Beauvoir's argument is that the situation of a housewife is more limiting than that of the person who works in the "real world." The "real world" may appear every bit as stultifying as the life of a housewife, but in the final analysis, if freedom is the ultimate criterion for all values, there is more freedom and a greater number of possibilities for the educated man than for a woman who has been limited to the confines of the home.

Our next concern is with the justification for the Aristotelean values that de Beauvoir holds. If freedom is the standard, why are the "masculine virtues" superior to "the feminine"? I believe that two sorts of argument can be given. First, one can argue that, on an individual basis, Aristotle's virtues equip the person to deal more adequately with the problems of the world and hence enhance the person's freedom. Secondly, one could argue that a society peopled with citizens who possessed Aristotle's virtues would enhance the growth of individual freedom.

We have seen that de Beauvoir's other values or character
traits were typically masculine virtues and ironically bore a
marked resemblance to the essentialist Aristotle's virtues.
Nowhere does de Beauvoir extol the typical feminine virtues of
being emotional, tender hearted, and sympathetic. Yet if
freedom is her ultimate value the reason for this is clear: to be
an emotional person is to lose control of oneself, to be a slave
to the passions, to be overcome, and to lose one's freedom. To
have a rational control of one's emotions is to do what one
wills, to be free. The emotions or passions have been criticized
from the time of the Greeks as being enemies to anyone who
desired freedom and independence. In Plato's Republic the tyrant
is characterized as the least free of all persons simply because
he is ruled by his passions and not his reason.[78] For Aristotle,
the slave is the person who follows his emotions or desires
because he lacks the rational ability to control his desires. He
reasoned that women too must be lacking in such a capacity,
simply because they did not seem to be able to control themselves.[79]
For St. Paul, the passions or desires are those qualities which
condemn humans to lives of sin, if they are not controlled by
the will.[80] Kant's distinction between the rational freedom
through which a person becomes a moral agent and the emotions or
passions which incline us away from choosing the ethical life is
yet another example of this point. De Beauvoir is simply operating
in this same tradition. Reason, self-control, courage, etc., are

all characteristics which aid one in manifesting one's freedom.
The emotions, if they are in control, take away one's ability to
act intelligently in the face of problems. Persons who are too
emotional become the slaves of uncontrollable powers which
supremely limit their effectiveness in dealing with problems in
the real world.

Not only does de Beauvoir extol the Aristotelean virtues,
but her analysis of the development of the feminine virtues in a
young girl shows that she, like Aristotle, believes that whatever
character traits one ends up with are a product of habit and
training. Women typically lack these traits which are so valuable
in attaining freedom because they are not allowed or encouraged
to exercise these capacities when young. Courage, self-control,
rational objectivity, critical thought, questioning, and creativity
are simply not encouraged. Rather, the young girl is encouraged
to be overconcerned for her appearance, to be passive, to show
her emotions (because this attracts the attention of the male),
to be concerned with household affairs, and not to be concerned
with the affairs of the world, or politics. By not exercising her
freedom she never knows she is an autonomous human being equipped
with all the powers with which men are equipped. She is a
dependent being because she is taught to be a dependent being.
It is by being dependent and adopting a passive disposition that
a woman becomes a "good wife," the slave to the husband. Her

success as a wife means to destroy her potential as a human
being. As de Beauvoir puts the issue, "...there is a contradiction between her status as a human being and her vocation
as a female."[81]

There is another argument which could be offered to explain
why the Aristotelean virtues are important to any person who
values the free development of human potentials. The development
of human potentials only occurs in a society. The society
provides the education, the security, and the colleagues through
which one can develop as a human being. One could simply ask
which kind of society would best allow for this development: a
society filled with citizens possessing the Aristotelean virtues
or a society filled with citizens possessing the feminine virtues?
The obvious needs but little discussion. Simply imagine a
society where half the people are irrational, emotional, dishonest,
weak, cowardly, passive persons and ask if it could provide the
education, security, and friendship (in the Aristotelean sense)
needed for proper human development. Could such a society fulfill
human needs as adequately as one where all members are relatively
rational, courageous, honest, active citizens? Along these same
lines J.S. Mill argued in "The Subjection of Women" that women
should be educated like men because this would in effect be
"doubling the mass of mental faculties available for the higher
service of humanity...there is such a deficiency of persons
competent to do excellently anything which it requires any

considerable amount of ability to do; that the loss to the world,
by refusing to make one-half of the whole quantity of talent it
possesses, is extremely serious."[82]

To question the validity of Mill's claim seems senseless.
If our freedom is more easily realized in a healthy society,
clearly the more individuals who contribute to the excellence of
the society, the healthier the social environment.

However, there are those who would no doubt argue that
within the class of behavior traits normally called 'the feminine
virtues,' that there are positive virtues for which all persons
should aim. They would point out that the tendency towards
concernful or nurturing behavior is surely a virtue. Yet de
Beauvoir argues that woman should replace such virtues with the
"masculine virtues" of cold calculating reason and aggressiveness,
and that women should give up these positive character traits
which all persons should acquire.[83] Other critics would point out
that certain psychological studies have shown that it is far
healthier to openly express one's emotions than continually to
hide them through self-control, like the 'typical male' tends to
do. The ideal person would combine the most desirable traits of
the male and those of the female. The result would be a kind of
"androgynous person." As Ann Ferguson says in her essay,
"Androgyny As An Ideal for Human Development," such a person would
have "the desire and ability to do socially meaningful work, as

well as the desire and ability to be autonomous, and to relate
lovingly to other human beings."[84]

Every class of mine that has read The Second Sex has voiced
similar objections. There seems to be a fear that de Beauvoir,
if she had her way, would do away with certain feminine characteristics which most feel are very important to the human race. Yet,
while there is some validity in such objections, I do not believe
that de Beauvoir is wholly guilty. I believe that one reason,
apart from the reasons already given in terms of human freedom,
that she seems to overemphasize the "masculine virtues" such as
aggressiveness and competitiveness is because of her ontology.
She believes that humans are by nature aggressive and that each
consciousness seeks to dominate the other. While this will be
discussed at length in the next chapter, it is enough here to
point out that if one adopts such an ontology, nurturing
behavior, as commonly understood, is not natural. When it occurs,
such behavior is but a veiled attempt to control the other. In
its place de Beauvoir emphasizes a kind of love which forces the
beloved to become more and more independent, the hardest love
that Nietzsche once said, "closes the open hand."

Secondly, with respect to the value of openly showing one's
emotions, I believe a case can be made that in certain instances
being open with one's feelings is a virtue, while in others, as
I have already argued, it is a weakness which destroys one's
ability to act. The kind of person of which de Beauvoir is

critical is the person who has the tendency to deal with all
stressful situations emotionally rather than rationally, not
the person who when overcome with grief openly shows his or her
pain. She is critical of the kind of person like Achilles in
The Iliad who bemoans the death of his friend Patroclus so long
and to such extremes that a large portion of the army of which he
is the leader is killed. Nowhere does she say that humans should
give up emotion and passion and replace them completely with
rationality. Only if the person replaces rationality with
emotion, which she feels women too often do, is she critical.

Thirdly, her critique of women being emotional is not a
critique of the emotions in general but is a critique of persons
who use emotional displays, as opposed to reason and argument,
to 'get their way.' While in many relationships such outbursts
may be even more effective than Socratic dialectic in manipulating
the behavior of others, the tragedy for women is that they tend
to rely solely upon these emotional outbursts. In doing this,
women do not develop the rational capacities which would be much
more useful in attaining success in the working world. As we
have seen, it is the lack of rational development which makes it
so difficult for women to compete effectively with men in the
'real world' outside of the home.

Hence, while de Beauvoir does emphasize the "masculine
virtues" to a great extent, I do not believe that she is telling
humans to give up their emotions and to quit caring for others in

a concernful way. (It seems obvious that it was primarily out of <u>concern</u> for the freedom of women that <u>The Second Sex</u> was written.) Rather she is saying that women who have effectively used emotional outbursts to achieve their goals need to realize that reason is a much more valuable tool. (The influence of <u>The Second Sex</u> on the women's movement clearly supports such a position.) And secondly, there are other ways to love and nurture a human being besides coddling and sheltering the person. As we have seen, one reason that young males develop the rational and aggressive tendencies which ultimately allow them to control the world is because parents, <u>out of love</u>, force them to realize these capacities. If the highest love is what benefits the beloved, which sort of 'nurturing' is ultimately the most beneficial?

4.) <u>Why Be Concerned With the Freedom of Others?</u>

We have examined the arguments for de Beauvoir's position that freedom is the ultimate value. We have also seen how the attainment of human freedom is enhanced by a person valuing the traditional masculine or Aristotelean virtues as opposed to the more feminine virtues. Our next concern is to see how de Beauvoir and Sartre might justify the move from the position that one ought to value individual freedom to the position that one ought to be concerned with the freedom of all. Or to put the question in terms of her feminism, why should the individual

woman, who values her own freedom, be concerned with the freedom
of all persons? Why should a woman adopt a position which is
other oriented rather than self oriented?

Before examining these questions, there is another concern
that some commentators have seen as undermining any attempt to
generate an ethics of concern for others by either Sartre or de
Beauvoir. Bernstein simply denies that Sartrean ethics is
possible because of Sartre's ontology, which characterizes the
essence of all human relations as "conflict." [85] According to
this position, concern for the well-being of other people is
ruled out by an ontology which holds that "When two human categories are together, each aspires to impose its sovereignty on
the other. Each tries to fulfill himself by reducing the other
to slavery."[86]

However Hobbesian this view of human nature may sound, others
have pointed out that although Sartre does hold this position,
a case can be made that he also believes humans can,
through an act of the will, overcome the disposition to oppress
others or to be God.[87] According to this interpretation, humans
may indeed be inclined towards the continual domination of other
consciousnesses, but because humans are free, their freedom can
choose not to value this inclination. It is possible to value
doing one's moral duty instead. The fact that something is
naturally desired does not entail that a person must choose to act
on that desire. It appears that de Beauvoir also holds this

position when she says in The Second Sex, "It is possible to
rise above conflict if each freely recognizes the other."[88]
However, such behavior never becomes 'second nature' as she says
that it is necessary for humans to continue making this choice
"without ceasing."[89]

Hence, if a person can through an act of free choice treat
others ethically, ethics is at least possible. The picture one
gets of human behavior is very Kantian, where human inclinations
and the rational will to do one's duty are most often diametri-
cally opposed and that one's true moral worth comes from the
rational will overcoming the inclination to oppress others.

Now, given that persons can overcome the tendency to oppress
others, the question which confronts de Beauvoir (and all persons
for that matter) is why should one show concern for the freedom
and well-being of others?

De Beauvoir does not argue that because human freedom is
the foundation of all values, and hence the ultimate good, and
because all persons by nature desire the good, that all persons
ought to desire freedom--not only their own freedom, but the
freedom of all persons. While she agrees with the conclusion of
such an argument, she does not argue in this way. Besides such
an argument committing the naturalistic fallacy, from an
existential perspective which holds that freedom and only freedom
is the ultimate value, one would always have to show why being
ethical or choosing to be such an ethical person would enhance one's

freedom. If acting ethically, and hence being concerned for the freedom of all persons, cannot be shown to aid one's freedom, then the choice would merely be an example of the myriad of choices that consciousness freely chooses. No compelling reasons could be given. Granted, if one did make the choice to live the role of an ethical person, quite apart from all concerns over one's self-interest, then one in some Kantian sense would surely have to be concerned with the welfare of other human beings. Yet, ultimately, I believe that de Beauvoir's position is one that does not presuppose that the person has already chosen to live the life of the ethical person, but rather is a person who simply wants to know why it would be in his or her self-interest to be concerned for the freedom of others. Let us examine this position.

First one should notice that Sartre and de Beauvoir believe that humans always choose what appears to be "the better."[90] So, if a person chooses to show concern for others, it must be because such a choice appears to be "the better" when compared to other possible choices. In support of this interpretation, Sartre says that we should be concerned for the freedom of others because our own freedom which we value is ultimately dependent upon their freedom.

> I declare that freedom, in respect to concrete
> circumstances can have no other end and aim but
> itself and when once a man has seen that values
> depend upon himself, in that state of forsakeness
> he can will only one thing, and that is freedom
> as the foundation of all values. That does not

> mean that he wills it in the abstract: it simply
> means that the actions of men of good faith have,
> as their ultimate significance, the quest of
> freedom itself, as such. A man who belongs to
> some communist or revolutionary society wills
> certain concrete ends, which imply the will to
> freedom, but that freedom is willed in the
> community. We will freedom for freedom's sake,
> in and through particular circumstances. And in
> thus willing freedom, we discover that it depends
> entirely upon the freedom of others and that the
> freedom of others depends upon our own.[91]
> (emphasis mine)

While Sartre's position may be clear, his reasoning is not
exactly self-evident. First he says that freedom is the ultimate
value. We have already seen why that is the case. Then he points
out that freedom, the freedom to realize oneself through action,
and "there is no reality except in action,"[92] is always in a
social community. We have already seen why this is the case
in our argument for the supremacy of the "masculine virtues." But
finally, he maintains that the ability to realize one's chosen
projects in the community is dependent on the freedom of others.
Why our freedom depends upon the freedom of others is far from
self-evident. Or simply put, why is the freedom of others
necessary for my own freedom? One can certainly imagine someone
like Aristotle living in a society which practiced slavery, who
at least appeared, by any commonly held standard, to have
freely realized his human potentials to a very high degree and
was not concerned with the oppression of slaves (in any other
sense than to give a rational justification for their oppression).

If, as in the case of Aristotle, one is a member of the oppressing
class and living a productive, self-fulfilling life, it is not
clear why it would be in one's own self-interest to seek the
freedom of the oppressed. Or if one is a member of an oppressed
class, but one benefits from the oppressing institution, as in the
case of some housewives of the upper class who benefit from
the institution of marriage and the traditional roles allotted to
women, it is not clear why one's freedom would be enhanced through
the destruction of the oppressing institutions. Further argument is needed in order to support Sartre's and de Beauvoir's
position.

Let us examine Sartre's attempt to solve the problem. He
holds that only within a social setting where all are free can
the individual realize his or her problem. Some Sartrean critics,
such as Thomas Anderson, try to support this position.[93] Anderson
argues that in order to engage in meaningful projects an individual
needs the help of others; "I cannot do much to bring the material
world under my control without joining forces with others."[94]
The individual can engage in free activities only if others allow
it, or if others provide the necessary social framework within
which one can carry out one's projects.

It seems to me that there is some truth in this position,
but clearly the argument does not show that the individual should
will the freedom of or be concerned with the well-being of all
human beings. If the security needed to carry on one's projects is

all one desires, one should no doubt will the freedom of those others who can aid in the security needed. It does not follow that one needs to be concerned about all people's freedom. In the case of the sexist society ruled by men, it may make perfectly good sense for men to will their own freedom as a class and, because they see that part of their freedom is tied to the oppression of women, not be concerned with freeing women. If men perceive that they benefit from women's serving them as housekeepers, mothers, and sex objects, why would they will the freedom of women? Or if an upper class housewife perceives that she benefits from the traditional institutions of marriage and motherhood, why should she be interested in opposing these institutions?

However, one might argue that one's safety is always in danger in such a class society because the oppressed class might rise up and destroy its oppressors. Women (the lesbian separatists) might ban together and violently overthrow their male oppressors. If this is the case it would appear to be in the interest of the ruling class to free the oppressed before the "dialectical inversion" occurs. While this may be true, it is not clear that the oppressing class will perceive this to be in their own interest. In the face of such a threat, they may simply choose to build up their own strength and oppress the others even more. If the oppressor believes that it is through his oppression that his most valued activities can be undertaken, he may rationally decide that it is in his best interest to continue the oppressive state. But

only if he clearly sees that his oppression of others is a real
threat to his own existence or to his interests, will he change.

Sartre, however, argues that to continue to allow oppression
of any is a threat to all people. In his Anti-Semite and Jew he
says,

> Anti-Semitism is a problem that affects us all
> directly...if we do not respect the person of the
> Israelite, who will respect us? If we are
> conscious of these dangers...we shall begin to
> understand that we must fight for the Jew, no
> more or no less than ourselves.[95]

Sartre's point is that our best defense against being the victim
of oppression is to fight for the freedom of all persons. Sartre
may be saying that by virtue of our own behavior, if we oppress
others or allow oppression, we are implying that oppression is
allowable. Only if one works for the freedom of others can one
consistently will that the others should help out if the
occasion should arise where one needs their help. Not to help
others achieve their freedom is to condone openly no one
helping anyone else to achieve freedom. Practically speaking,
this could be a disastrous position to take if one ever did need
the help of others. The application of the "Golden Rule" to the
oppressor or to the one who refuses to help the oppressed would
entail that the oppressing person could not expect help from
others.

While this may be Sartre's position, I believe there are
still problems. As Thomas Anderson points out, Sartre seems to

be presupposing a rather Kantian notion when he argues for equal
rights of all persons.[96] But according to Anderson, Sartre

> implies that consistency demands that all freedom
> be valued equally, since all men are equal inas-
> much as no one possesses any ontological superiority
> over another - for all lack intrinsic value...But
> I see ultimately no reason to concede to Sartre that
> the equality of all men means that I must choose to
> value all freedoms equally. I see no contradiction
> in admitting on one hand that all men are equal,
> that none possess intrinsic value, yet choosing to
> value my own freedom...I could fully recognize
> that it possesses no intrinsic right to be
> singled out, and yet prefer it (because)...my
> freedom and no one else's is the source of all my
> values and meaning.[97]

Basically, I agree with Anderson's criticism. It seems to
me that Sartre here presupposes that the person who recognizes the
equality of all persons has chosen to value the point of view
of Kantian ethics. Why, from the existentialist perspective
concerning values, should a person choose to value such a point
of view? Why couldn't the person simply recognize that all persons
are equal and still choose to oppress others when he or she felt
it was in his or her own best interest? It is true, however,
as Plato pointed out in his Republic, that in the extreme case of
egoism the tyrannical man is always in danger for his life.[98]
But in the case of women's oppression, we are not dealing with
tyrants. We are dealing with relatively "normal" people who have
chosen rather traditional roles and choose to turn their backs
on the oppression which exists for over one-half the members of
their society; i.e., women. Such a person simply perceives that it

is his or her best interest to support the interest of the powerful oppressing class of which he or she is a member or which benefits that person. The person is not openly a tyrant, but merely a person who has chosen a non-revolutionary role and quietly goes about his or her own business looking out for what appears to that person to be "the better." The person would have had to have chosen as a fundamental project that of "being an ethical being above all else," before the moral argument concerning one's duty to all human being's freedom would have been compelling.

Let us return to Sartre's position in "Existentialism is a Humanism." I believe that Sartre is correct in pointing out that people need others to fulfill their desires, and that it makes good pragmatic sense to will the freedom of those one needs. However, he has not shown that it is in one's best interest to will the freedom of all or that all need to be free in order for the individual to realize his potential. However, I think a more plausible argument can be constructed when we keep in mind what de Beauvoir's position in terms of women is in The Second Sex.

Let us return to the notion that we ought to help others because only in helping others can we expect the aid of others if the situation should arise where we need the help. Sartre's and de Beauvoir's position, especially in terms of the liberation of women, might be construed as follows: Although the individual woman

may not presently perceive that freeing all women is in her best
interest, if she were to see that in the long run certain
changes in the society would in fact benefit her, and that these
changes involved the rights of all women, she would work for such
changes. For example, if women saw that, even though they were
presently being taken care of by a well-to-do husband, there
was a good chance that before they die they would have to care for
themselves, they would see that indeed the liberation of all
women for meaningful jobs and adequate pay was in their own best
interests. If women knew that the odds were that they would be
divorced or widowed and hence would have to support themselves,
they would not will that women remain in their present state of
dependency and inequality.[99] The attitude of 'Oh well, it'll
never happen to me' which keeps women from engaging in the struggle
for freedom of all would be replaced by a kind of activism. One
might say that no rational person who knew that the odds were
the person would need to be self-supporting at some time
would choose to support institutions which made such support
nearly impossible. It would be like playing Russian roulette
with four of six bullets in the chamber. If all choose what
appears "the better," self-sufficiency is clearly better than
poverty and dependence.

While we are not arguing for any sort of Kantian notion of
ethical duty, but simply from practical concerns with reference
to self-interest, Kant's example of the person who is considering

making it a universal law that no person helps another may help illustrate the problem. This example deals with a person who is very wealthy and feels perfectly secure. Hence, because of the feeling of security, the person was willing to adopt a moral law or principle which precluded anyone helping anyone else. Even in this situation, Kant thought that such a rational person would see that it was not in his or her best interest to will such a law. The slightest chance, or mere logical possibility, of needing the help of another was enough for Kant to think that no rational human being would will a universal law that no one helps anyone else.[100] In the case of women, or most human beings, the security and wealth present in Kant's example are marginal or missing. The need to ensure the freedom of all women should be evident to any woman who understands the situation.

Part of the problem may be that it is not clear what Sartre means when he says that one _ought_ to work for the freedom of _all_. First, the argument has shown that the 'ought' here is not the _moral_ ought; it is the ought of enlightened self-interest. Secondly, what does it mean to work for the "freedom of all"? One way to look at it is for a person to be a good Samaritan who is always doing good deeds for other particular people. However, if it is interpreted as such, working for the freedom of others may not be in one's best interest, especially if there is no heaven or hell. On the other hand, if working for the freedom of others means to be engaged in political struggles to change laws and institutions which limit our freedom and the freedom of others, this could be more easily defended. De Beauvoir claims in the introduction to The Second Sex that it is the "institutions" which limit human freedom in terms of "concrete opportunities." It is these institutions which she opposes.[101] Her concern for the freedom of all women is a concern for restructuring the prevailing social institutions, such as marriage, which limit the possibilities for women as a class. Her individual freedom is attained only by working to change the society at the political level, not by working to free the individual. From de Beauvoir's perspective, the freedom one has is a function of the social structure in which one lives.

Thus, while it may be questionable whether an individual will perceive that working for the freedom of others on an individual level is in that person's best interests, it is clear that once the individual perceives him or herself as a member of a class of persons whose freedom could be enhanced by certain political or institutional changes, that person would perceive that such political changes were ultimately beneficial to his or her own freedom. If every person wills what appears "the better," which means that which with high probability will benefit that person, opposition to such changes would only occur due to either ignorance or some masochistic tendency.

If we are to confine the issue to women's liberation as construed by de Beauvoir, then the counter-example of someone like

Aristotle, who belongs to the ruling class as a highly educated
male and is self-sufficient, is not really appropriate. While
someone like Aristotle may someday need the help of others, the
chances are that he won't. But in the case of women, with the
divorce rate as high as it is and the fact that women live longer
than men, the chances are very high that any woman will have to
support herself financially at some time in her life. Hence it
is clearly in any woman's best interest to work for the freedom
of all women by opposing any institution which stands in the way
of financial independence for women; i.e., marriage and its
traditional sex-related roles.

It would also seem that men too, as a class of persons, would,
upon a closer examination of the situation, perceive that the
liberation of women was in their own best interest. There are
reasons which deal with sexuality and marital relations which will
be discussed in the next chapter. But there are also economic
reasons. If the man desires financial security, the more his wife
can earn in the job market the higher the economic standard and
security of the family as a whole. Secondly, the more a woman
earns, the less financial pressure there is on the husband to be
the "bread winner." In such a situation, the man would be freed
from many of the typical anxieties over losing his job. Thirdly,
as we saw in de Beauvoir's chapter on motherhood, working mothers
who are self-sufficient make better mothers. According to de
Beauvoir, such women have far more to offer their children and ask

for little in return.[102] Of course the husband in such a situation must be willing to give up his dominant role as oppressor. But as we have seen, this would really be to his advantage.

Apart from these practical reasons as to why it makes good sense to work for the freedom of others through restructuring or eliminating the oppressive institutions, a different sort of argument based on de Beauvoir's ontology could be constructed. We have already seen that de Beauvoir takes it as a given that human beings seek recognition from other human beings. This recognition cannot be forced recognition; otherwise we end up with Hegel's master-slave relation where the master soon realizes that the recognition from the slave is of little value, simply because the honor and recognition is forced. The slave gives it only because he or she fears for his or her life; it is not freely given out of admiration. What persons desire is the free recognition of others, and this is only possible if the other is free and understands the merit of the person's work. The tragedy of the master is that the slave cannot appreciate the master's worth (if he has any) nor can the slave freely give the needed recognition. We have seen that the same problem arises in de Beauvoir's work in her analysis of the traditional relations between husbands and wives and between mothers and their children. Human beings desire freely given recognition and honor from other humans who can appreciate their work (which for de Beauvoir means their projects). The typical wife, lacking experience in the world, cannot

understand the man's projects in work, and the child in its naive
state cannot comprehend the merit of the mother. In addition,
both wife and child are not free persons but dependent. Thus,
their recognition is, relatively speaking, of little value.

However, a skeptic to such thinking might point out that
many persons appear to attain a great deal of pleasure and satisfaction from the honor and recognition of those who are not their
equals. For example, many teachers find the admirations of their
students to be quite rewarding. Many parents find the love and
respect given by their children to be very important. Most
entertainers find the applause of their fans to be very pleasurable.
Hence, why should one believe that recognition is valuable only
if it comes from one's peers or equals?

While such examples clearly exist and no one would argue with
their truth, I believe that one can effectively argue, as Socrates
does in the Republic with reference to the various levels of
pleasure, that only the person who has experienced the honor given
him by fans, family, students, and peers can judge where the
most pleasure or meaning lies. If all humans desire recognition,
then any recognition is better than none at all. If a woman,
barred from the world of work lacks all means to direct social
recognition, it seems only natural that she would believe that the
love and devotion of her family were ultimately the most rewarding
things in the world. Or, in the case of the teacher, if the
teacher's merits are not recognized by his or her peers, it is

only natural that the praise of his or her students would have extreme value. The same argument would apply to an entertainer. If peer recognition is not tremendously rewarding, why do musicians place so much value on the honors awarded by the music industry--such as the Grammy Awards? It seems to me that de Beauvoir's position is correct. To use an example from J.S. Mill, of course those who have only experienced 'pig pleasures' will argue that such experiences are the epitome of human experiences. But those who have experienced both kinds, 'the pig and the human,' will testify that the human pleasures are higher.

If we accept de Beauvoir's position, two points follow. First, if one desires the free recognition of others, the others must be free. And secondly, if the value of the recognition of the other is proportional to how well the other person understands our projects, then the more of an equal or superior the other is, the greater the worth of the recognition. In the example of teaching, a professor does not value the praise of his or her students as much as that of his or her colleagues simply because the students are not equal in their understanding of the professor's ideas when compared to the understanding of his or her colleagues. (As someone once said, "The one eyed man is king in the land of the blind!") It follows from this that if one desires recognition from others, the others should be both free and at least one's equal. Thus to achieve such recognition, one should work to free others from a state of dependency and strive to make them equal in terms of the understanding necessary for cogent judgment. As Anderson points out, "...it would be inconsistent with his desire for personal justification for a man to refuse to value the freedom of others and to prevent them from or not assist them in becoming his equals."[103] Only one's peers can give one the needed recognition, so in order to maximize the possibility of this recognition, one should work to make all persons at least capable of being one's peers. Or to put it another way, because one's value as a human being is dependent upon the freedom of others, the freedom of others should be one's primary concern.

No matter how convincing this argument appears, the case of the man like Aristotle keeps creeping in as a counter-example. De Beauvoir's position is that one can maximize one's own value by valuing the freedom of all persons, seeking to make all persons free equal human beings, and seeking to make all persons one's peers. But in the case of Aristotle (and others like him) what is desired is not the recognition of all persons. Aristotle realized that all humans were probably not capable of understanding and appreciating the merit of his work. He desired the friendship and recognition of the "select few."[104] It was clear to him that all persons were not of equal understanding and to seek honor from the ignorant was not desirable for a man of virtue. Thus it appears that for some people, what is desired is not the recognition of all people but merely the recognition of a few. It would follow that one should work for the freedom and understanding of those whose judgment one would value, but not for the freedom of all. As Anderson points out, why should one be concerned about the freedom of those members of a planet "who will never know his name?"[105]

I believe that one could point out in defense of de Beauvoir's position that the person like Aristotle who is concerned for the freedom of and recognition from the select few, holds that position because he believes only a few people are capable "by nature" of the understanding needed for intelligent recognition. De Beauvoir might well argue that what she is concerned with is giving all people the freedom for developing their rational capacities through institutional changes in the oppressive society. To will the freedom of all because one desires to maximize the possibility of peer recognition simply means that the number of possible peers can only be known once all have been given an equal opportunity to realize their intellectual and moral faculties. There can be no a priori grounds for not equally valuing all person's freedom. Only after all have been given equal opportunity might the person like Aristotle choose to value the opinions of some over the opinions of others.

When this argument is combined with the previous one which showed that no rational person should choose to support an institution or political system which would make it impossible for him or her to become self-sufficient, should the need arise, de Beauvoir's position that one ought to be concerned with the freedom

of all seems well-founded. Unfortunately she does not clearly
give the arguments, but I believe one can see that they are implied
in her critiques of such traditional institutions as marriage, of
the life of the upper class housewife, and of the normal practices
in educating female children to be housewives and hence second
class citizens.

IV. Summary and Conclusion

We have seen that many of the objections that could be aimed
at de Beauvoir's value system can be answered once one grounds her
values not merely on capricious choice, but on the condition for
the possibility of choice: human freedom. Once the argument that
if anything has value, freedom, as the ground of all values, must
have value has been explicated, it is but a short step to see
why de Beauvoir is critical of any institution that tends to destroy
human freedom. Her next move is to show how the life of the
typical housewife/mother destroys such freedom, while on the
other hand, the male "Aristotelean" virtues enhance one's ability
to realize one's freedom in the world. Hence, given such an argument, I believe she is quite right in extolling these "masculine
virtues" over the "feminine" character traits.

Housework is not only an instance of alienated labor; it is
an instance which supremely limits human freedom. The life of a
housewife is not merely an instance of bad faith; it is an instance
of bad faith which makes the woman who chooses that role totally

212

dependent upon her husband, thus limiting her freedom even more. This is why de Beauvoir holds that until women are not allowed to make the choice to be a housewife and mother, women will never be truly equal to men.

I suppose there are persons who would still argue that if a person wants freely to choose to become a slave, one has a perfect right to do so, and that de Beauvoir has no right to impose her values on such persons. De Beauvoir's response would no doubt be that such a choice is immoral because by making such a choice, the person is implicitly endorsing such behavior. The person is saying to others that "It is okay to be a slave (housewife)." Although, if all persons involved have complete knowledge of the situation, whether they choose to follow the person's example or not may be their own business. But, the children involved with that person do not have complete knowledge of the situation. It is the influence upon the child that is problematic. The child is instinctively drawn towards "imitating" its parent. This ensures that the institution which denies human freedom will continue to exist. The mother is implicitly telling the child that it is perfectly acceptable to be a housewife. This is one reason why de Beauvoir is so intent on doing away with the institution.

If a fully grown woman wants to choose to be a housewife and if the consequences of such a choice were known, and if the woman did not care what kind of an example she was setting for her children, de Beauvoir would probably say that the choice was immoral and irrational but if the woman wanted to be an immoral fool that was her business.

The problem is that as long as many women make the choice, it appears to be a perfectly natural role for women to choose. Hence the feminist who is critical of such behaviors will appear "unnatural" or as a radical. A life of oppression becomes the "natural" way for women. To oppose what is thought "natural" is always difficult.

FOOTNOTES

[1]Jeanson, Sartre and the Problem of Morality, p. XXXIX.

[2]SS 673.

[3]Sartre, EH, p. 291.

[4]Ibid.

[5]SS 53.

[6]SS 302-303.

[7]Richard Bernstein, Praxis and Action (Philadelphia: University of Pennsylvania Press, 1971), p. 142.

[8]de Beauvoir, Force of Circumstance, p. 67.

[9]BN 38.

[10]BN 481-489.

[11]BN 626.

[12]BN 627.

[13]Mary Warnock, Existential Ethics (London: Macmillan, 1967), pp. 47-48.

[14]SS XXXII.

[15]Ibid.

[16]Aristotle, Nichomachean Ethics, in The Basic Works of Aristotle, Ed. Richard McKeon (New York: Random House, 1941), Bk. I, Chapter 13. Future references to Aristotle are taken from The Basic Works of Aristotle.

[17]Aristotle, Metaphysics, in The Basic Works of Aristotle, Book I, Chapter 1.

[18]Aristotle, Nichomachean Ethics, in The Basic Works of Aristotle, Bk. X, Ch. 7.

[19]John Stuart Mill, "Utilitarianism," in The Essential Works of John Stuart Mill (New York: Bantam, 1971), pp. 195-197.

[20]John Stuart Mill, "The Subjection of Women," in Women in Western Thought, Ed. Martha Osborne (New York: Random House, 1979), p. 280.

[21]Ibid., p. 279.

[22]J.S. Mill, "On Liberty," in The Essential Works of J.S. Mill, p. 262.

[23]SS XXXIII.

[24]Ibid.

[25]Ibid.

[26]Ibid.

[27]Aristotle, Nichomachean Ethics, Bk. IX, Ch. 7, 1168a.

[28]op. cit., Bk. I, Ch. 5, 1098a.

[29]Ibid., Bk. X, Ch. 4, 1174b, 15-20.

[30]Ibid., Bk. X, Chps. 7-8.

[31]SS 334.

[32]SS 697.

[33]SS 698.

[34]Aristotle, op. cit., Bk. X, Ch. 6, 1176b, 35.

[35]$\underline{SS}$ 672.

[36]Aristotle, <u>Nichomachean Ethics</u>, Bk. IV, Ch. 4.

[37]$\underline{SS}$, Chap. XXI, pp. 663-698.

[38]$\underline{SS}$ 376.

[39]$\underline{SS}$ 666.

[40]$\underline{SS}$ 553.

[41]Aristotle, <u>Metaphysics</u>, Bk. 1, Ch. 1, 980.

[42]Mill, "Utilitarianism," p. 221.

[43]Jean-Paul Sartre, <u>The Critique of Dialectical Reason</u>. Trans. Alan Sheridan-Smith (London: NLB, 1978), p. 90.

[44]In contemporary feminist literature, there is an interesting and insightful analysis of this phenomena in women in Collette Dowling's book <u>The Cinderella Complex</u> (New York: Simon and Schuster, 1981). She argues that women in fact do not desire freedom. Rather than desiring independence, they desire to be taken care of. Regardless of all the talk about women's liberation, she says women tend to desire the security afforded them in traditional roles, even though this is a false security. To truly take responsibility for one's life is typically avoided at all costs by women. However, she agrees with de Beauvoir that this is not because women by nature seek security, but because they are taught to believe that it is all right to be taken care of by man.

[45]Sartre, <u>EH</u>, p. 307.

[46]Simone de Beauvoir, <u>The Ethics of Ambiguity</u>. Trans. Bernard Gretchman (Secaucus, N.J.: Citadel Press, 1949), p. 24.

[47]Mill, "Utilitarianism," p. 192, 220.

[48]Aristotle, <u>Posterior Analytics</u>, in <u>The Basic Works of Aristotle</u>, Bk. II, Ch. 19.

[49]Wilfred Desan, The Marxism of Jean-Paul Sartre (Garden City, N.Y.: Doubleday and Co. Inc., 1966), p. 4.

[50]Simone de Beauvoir, "Literature et Metaphysique," quoted in Wilfred Desan, The Tragic Finale (New York: Harper and Row, 1960), p. 7.

[51]John Wild, Existence and the World of Freedom (Englewood Cliffs, N.J.: Prentice-Hall, 1965), p. 42.

[52]SS 668.

[53]Sartre, EH, p. 303.

[54]See Thomas Anderson, The Foundation and Structure of Sartrean Ethics (Lawrence, Ks.: Regents Press of Kansas, 1979), p. 79.

[55]See Karl Popper, Conjectures and Refutations (New York: Harper & Row, 1965), pp. 33-65.

[56]SS 418, 420, 444.

[57]SS XXXIII.

[58]Jeanson, Sartre and the Problem of Morality, p. XXXIX.

[59]SS XXXIII.

[60]BN L1.

[61]BN 88-89.

[62]BN 627.

[63]BN 435-436.

[64]BN 433-441.

[65]SS 434.

[66]<u>SS</u> XXXIII.

[67]David Hume, <u>Treatise on Human Nature</u> (London: Oxford Press, 1973), pp. 468-469.

[68]<u>BN</u> 38.

[69]<u>SS</u> 40-41.

[70]de Beauvoir, <u>The Ethics of Ambiguity</u>, p. 24.

[71]Anderson, <u>The Foundation and Structure of Sartrean Ethics</u>, p. 47.

[72]Bernstein, <u>Praxis and Action</u>, pp. 153-154.

[73]Anderson, <u>op</u>. <u>cit</u>., p. 51.

[74]In fact, de Beauvoir holds that there is nothing more boring than works of art produced by housewives. Because they have done nothing, they seldom have anything to say. Their works are as boring as their lives.

[75]<u>SS</u> 762.

[76]<u>SS</u> 694.

[77]<u>SS</u> 778.

[78]Plato, <u>Republic</u>, Bk. IX.

[79]Aristotle, <u>Politics</u>, Bk. I.

[80]St. Paul, <u>Letter to the Romans</u>, 7:14-25.

[81]<u>SS</u> 376.

[82]Mill, "The Subjection of Women," p. 267.

[83] See Emma Goldman, "The Tragedy of Women's Emancipation,"
in The Feminist Papers. Ed. Alice Rossi (New York: Columbia
University Press, 1973), pp. 508-516; and Theodora Roszak,
"The Hard and the Soft: The Force of Feminism in Modern Times,"
in Masculine/Feminine. Eds. Betty and Theodore Roszak (New
York: Harper and Row, 1969), pp. 87-104.

[84] Ann Ferguson, "Androgyny As an Ideal for Human Development," Philosophy and Women (Belmont: Wadsworth, 1979), p. 46.

[85] Bernstein, Praxis and Action, pp. 153-155.

[86] SS 69, 158; see also Being and Nothingness, p. 429. "The
essence of the relations between consciousness is not Mitsein;
it is conflict."

[87] Anderson, The Foundation and Structure of Sartrean Ethics,
pp. 20-27; Gary Shapiro, "Choice and Universality in Sartre's
Ethics, Man and World, Vol. 7, No. 1, Feb. 1974, pp. 20-36.

[88] SS 158.

[89] Ibid.

[90] Sartre, EH, p. 292.

[91] Ibid., p. 307.

[92] Ibid., p. 300.

[93] See Thomas Anderson, "Is Sartrean Ethics Possible?",
Philosophy Today, Vol. 14, 1970, pp. 128-130.

[94] Ibid., p. 128.

[95] Jean-Paul Sartre, Anti-Semite and Jew. Trans. G. Becher.
(New York: Shocken, 1948), p. 151.

[96] Anderson, The Foundation and Structure of Sartrean Ethics,
p. 86.

[97] Ibid., p. 92.

[98]Plato, Republic, Bk. IX.

[99]See Collette Dowling, The Cinderella Complex, pp. 39-44. Dowling points out that women tend never to think about what will happen to them when they are forced to support themselves in old age or though a divorce. She points out that in 1977, the median income of all older females was $59 a week. This fact alone should make all women more than ready to work for their liberation from being dependent upon their husbands and attaining equal pay in the work force.

[100]See also John Rawls, The Theory of Justice (Cambridge: Belkamp, 1971).

[101]SS XXXIII.

[102]SS 573, 586.

[103]Anderson, The Foundation and Structure of Sartrean Ethics, p. 88.

[104]Aristotle, Nichomachean Ethics, Bk. IX, Ch. 10.

[105]Anderson, op. cit., p. 95.

CHAPTER IV

PROBLEMS WITH CONJUGAL LOVE:
SOCIAL AND ONTOLOGICAL

I. Introduction

In chapter two, we examined de Beauvoir's position that marriage tends to destroy a woman's self-development by condemning her to a life of alienated labor and bad faith. However, these problems do not exhaust de Beauvoir's criticism of the institution. As we saw, one of the major problems for women within the traditional institution of marriage has to do with the quality of her emotional relationship to her husband. To put the issue quite simply: according to de Beauvoir, men and women have trouble loving one another within the traditional institution of marriage. Married life is the antithesis of love.

As I understand de Beauvoir's position, the problems confronting the relationship can be divided into two kinds. First there are problems that arise because of the nature of the marital institution itself. In this case, certain changes in the institution and/or the structure of society might remedy these problems. The second sort of problem has to do with de Beauvoir's ontology. Here, although she often speaks of the nature and possibility of an ideal love relationship, it is my position that her ontology makes love or friendship, as commonly understood, impossible. The problem is explaining how, if one holds the position that the primary relationship between two consciousnesses is conflict or antagonism, love as a genuine caring and concern is possible. Even though she believes that consciousness can, through an act of sheer will, choose to deny its antagonistic propensity and treat others with care and concern, I do not believe that loving another person, as normally understood, is the same as doing one's duty or simply choosing to behave in a kindly fashion towards the other. While acting out of duty or commitment is an important aspect of friendship or love relations, commitment without an emotionally based feeling of care and good will towards the other is not love as generally understood.

Before discussing the possible solutions to these two problems, it may be helpful if we first get reasonably clear on de Beauvoir's idea of love. Then we can go on to examine the nature and causes of the problems. And finally we can analyze the proposed solutions offered by de Beauvoir.

It is my position that de Beauvoir's ontology precludes any notion of love between human beings that might include a spontaneous feeling of care and concern for the other's well-being. However, within the context of her discussion of love in The Second Sex, it may be the case that alternate explanations for human relations of good will can be generated. Interestingly enough, such alternative accounts of love, based on her Sartrean ontology may do a good deal to demystify love and in turn redefine the notion so that many of the problems for women which are created by the traditional idea of romantic love are overcome.

Regardless of how interesting this alternative account of love might be, I believe that there is a basic inconsistency between de Beauvoir's ontological view of human relations and the general notion of love that she employs throughout most of her analysis. That is to say, on one hand she criticizes typical marital relations because marriage tends to undermine the possibility for genuine care and concern between husband and wife, while at the same time she subscribes to an ontology which literally makes such concernful relations impossible. This, as I perceive it, is the fundamental weakness of The Second Sex.

II. De Beauvoir's Notion of Conjugal Love

There is not any place in The Second Sex where de Beauvoir succinctly tells her readers what she means by conjugal love. She consistently claims that marriage tends to destroy conjugal love, but she never clearly defines the idea.[1] Due to this shortcoming, I would like to propose the following working definition as one which at least provides some of the necessary conditions for whatever more complex notion de Beauvoir might have in mind: love is an emotional relation with another person such that the other is seen as a friend and is also erotically desired. The three important elements in such a definition are friendship, erotic

224

desire, and the notion of an emotional link to the other. I
believe that such a definition is consistent with what de Beauvoir
says throughout The Second Sex. Whenever she attacks the institution of marriage in terms of its destructiveness to human
relations, she either attacks it for killing the erotic, or she
attacks it for making friendship between husband and wife nearly
impossible.[2] Hence, it appears that friendship and erotic desire
are at least two essential parts of de Beauvoir's notion of love.
The final aspect of this definition is that love, as an emotional
relationship, cannot be willed. That is to say that love, as a
desire or sentiment, is different from acting out of sheer
commitment or duty. That she believes such sentiment to be important is evident when she is openly critical of women who marry
out of cold, calculated choice, as opposed to "love." One falls
in love; one does not will to fall in love. The emotional
response to the other is involuntary. (That is not to say
one must always act upon one's emotional stirrings.)

There may be other elements in her notion of love, but I
believe that these three are all necessary conditions and, while
perhaps not exhaustive, will suffice for an understanding of her
critique of love in marriage.

Such a definition also coincides with our everyday understanding of conjugal love, as well as the understanding of many
contemporary feminists. We would think it strange if a man said
that he loved his wife, but did not consider her to be his friend.

Someone might rightly correct the man and say, 'You mean you lust after your wife? How can one love another and not feel that the other is a friend?' In the reverse sense, we do not generally say we love a person and desire to marry that person unless we not only see the person as a friend but also desire that person sexually. While it may not be the quintessential element, erotic desire is at least a very important part of conjugal love. On the other hand, it is not a part of parental love or love for humanity.[3] (agape)

Let us examine the two qualities of friendship and erotic desire more closely in order to see why de Beauvoir believes that marriage destroys them. De Beauvoir's notion of friendship is not at all new or difficult since, like many of her other values, it appears to be taken directly from Aristotle.[4] Aristotle held the position that true friendship could only exist between equals.[5] In his ideal friendship between equals each person equally benefits the other in terms of utility, pleasure, or virtue. Hence, in Athens at that time, such friendship could only occur between men, given that Aristotle thought women and children were inherently unequal to men. Each member of the relationship wishes the best for the other, which according to Aristotle is the desire to instill a virtuous character in the other.[6] This is accomplished through a critical and dialectical relationship where each helps the other to achieve the highest human potential. Being reciprocal, the relationship benefits each in two ways. First, each wishes well

for the other and is benefitted by the other's acts, and secondly,
when each acts to bring about the best for the other, such
behavior benefits the actor by developing his disposition towards
virtuous action. Hence, while each benefits from the actions of
the friend, more importantly for Aristotle, each develops a
morally virtuous character through acting well towards the other.[7]

There are two lesser varieties of friendship for Aristotle,
each based on what he considers a less worthy desire than the
desire for the good of another. One is a relationship based on
utility; that is, one is friendly to another simply because of the
usefulness of the other. As Aristotle says, "Now those who love
each other for their utility do not love each other for themselves, but in virtue of some good which they get from each
other."[8] They are friends because of what they get from each
other. And as the usefulness changes, so does the friendship;
"...when the motive of the friendship is done away, the friendship
is dissolved."[9] The other lesser kind of friendship is that
based upon pleasure. Two people may be friends simply because
each brings pleasure to the other. This pleasure is typically an
emotional response to the other and may be the feeling associated
with what we today call "romantic love" prevalent among the
young. As Aristotle says, "...the friendship of young people
seems to aim at pleasure; for they live under the guidance of
emotion, and pursue above all what is pleasant to themselves and
what is immediately before them...Young people are amorous...the

greater part of the friendship of love depends on emotion and aims at pleasure; this is why they fall in love and quickly fall out of love...."[10]

For Aristotle, both of the elements of the lesser varieties of friendship, usefulness and pleasure, are important elements of any higher friendship. Clearly the friends who wish well for each other are also useful to each other and try to give each other pleasure, but their usefulness exceeds any immediate goals such as might exist between business partners who are friends simply because they share a common goal. In the same sense, the pleasure derived from the higher kind of relationship goes beyond particular amusements. It is the pleasure of each being helped and helping the other achieve his or her highest potential.

De Beauvoir's notion of friendship is much like Aristotle's. She believes that the true friend wishes the best for the other and helps the other achieve his or her proper excellence through dialectically forcing the friend to grow. As she says toward the end of The Second Sex, "An individual who is loved as a free being, in his humanity, is regarded with critical, demanding severity which is the other side of genuine esteem."[11] Like Plato, she knows that the fawning flatterer is no friend. Like Aristotle, she believes that for persons to be friends the persons must be equal. For a woman to love a man "she must believe herself his equal and be so in concrete fact."[12]

Freedom, equality, and critical severity are all parts of her notion of friendship. If any of these qualities is missing, the marital relationship may be a friendship based wholly on utility or perhaps sexual need, but not a true friendship. In fact, de Beauvoir believes that it is out of utility that women generally do get married, and she is critical of such decisions.[13] In such instances, the marital relation is like a business contract. The woman is hired to clean the man's house, cook the meals, raise his children, and provide sexual pleasure. In such a relation, the housewife is like a paid laborer/prostitute. "The only difference between women who sell themselves in prostitution and those who sell themselves in marriage is in the price and the length of time the contract runs."[14] The woman is hired for life, and the price is usually cheap. Such a relationship is clearly not what de Beauvoir (or anyone) means by love or the friendship that is essential to love.

When one understands what de Beauvoir means by friendship and how friendship requires mutual freedom, equality, and a kind of critical severity towards the other, it is easy to see why she is critical of the normal notion of romantic love where one or the other members of the relationship is elevated to the level of a near god in the eyes of the other. If a young girl sees her lover as the Prince Charming or a 'fallen God', she has destroyed all hope of the needed equality necessary for friendship. Besides that, such a woman is bound to be disappointed when her idolatry becomes reality through marriage and she finds that her 'fallen God' has feet of clay. In the same sense, de Beauvoir is critical of the young man who places his wife or mistress on a pedestal. A woman on a pedestal does not work. If she is allowed to work, this makes sure that the needed equality and independence achieved through a woman's labor are not present. Hence a true friendship between the two people is impossible as long as inequality continues.

All of this talk of friendship, equality, and freedom is not to say that de Beauvoir overlooks the importance of sexual desire and pleasure. As we have seen, she spends many pages describing and analyzing the problems of attaining sexual fulfillment within the institution of marriage.[15] From all of her efforts to understand the erotic, one could surely conclude that she saw it as an important element of conjugal love, an important element all too often missing in a marriage.

One thing is evident concerning de Beauvoir's view of the erotic: there is more to erotic pleasure than mere physical stimulation. It is more than what Alan Goldman has characterized as the "desire for contact with another person's body and for the pleasure which such contact produces."[16] For de Beauvoir, sexual pleasure must include an emotional element such that the two people actually care for each other. She is critical of those people who believe that erotic pleasure will follow from simply finding a person with whom to have sex and then reading a "how to

manual." "...sexual pleasure is not only a matter of technique."[17]
There must be care and concern beyond the physical attraction.
As she says, "in a genuinely moral erotic relation there is free
assumption of desire and pleasure;...this is possible only when the
other is recognized as an individual, in love or in desire."[18]
Without this love and recognition as a person, "the relation of
the two partners is no more than an animal relation."[19] When this
happens, she claims that sex is obscene. The human element of the
erotic has disappeared.

Thus the third element is introduced into de Beauvoir's
notion of love. Besides friendship and erotic desire for the
other, there is an emotional element of "love" for the other. The
person must have some sort of "amorous inclinations" such that
each desires the other, but the desire is for the well-being and
pleasure of the other as opposed to mere animal desire for sexual
contact. As de Beauvoir says, "love is an outgoing movement, an
impulse towards another person."[20] But it must seek to leave the
other person free, not to confine or coerce the person.[21]

An important aspect of this final element of love is that
as an "impulse" or "desire" for the other, it is an emotion or
sentiment. If it is an emotion, its existence is beyond the
control of the rational will. That is why we say that one "falls
in love," rather than that one chooses to love. If this amorous
inclination is missing, love does not exist. We may still have
what de Beauvoir calls "acceptance" but not love.[22]

In summary, we have seen that de Beauvoir's notion of
conjugal love contains three essential elements. First, there
is the notion of friendship which is a "dynamic relationship"[23]
between people who are free, equal, and willing to evaluate
critically each other for the sake of the personal growth of the
other. Second, love contains an erotic element in terms of sexual
desire for the other. And thirdly, there is an emotional element
such that each spontaneously seeks the well-being of the other,
and this element is essential for a meaningful erotic relationship.

III. Institutional Problems and Solutions

Now that we are reasonably clear on de Beauvoir's notion of
the ideal conjugal love, let us briefly reexamine her descriptions
of love within the institution of marriage in order to see again
why marriage destroys this ideal. If two conditions for love
are friendship and erotic desire, we need only to see how
marriage tends to destroy both. Once the problem is clear, then
we can examine possible solutions.

Let us begin with de Beauvoir's notion of the erotic. She
characterizes "good sex" as spontaneous erotic desire between
two free persons who mutually desire and respect each other.[24]
There are two problems with having such an experience within the
institution of marriage. First, marriage does not promote the
necessary equality and freedom. And secondly, marriage destroys
the spontaneous element of the erotic. As we saw in Chapter II,
according to de Beauvoir, the institution of marriage turns sexual

relations into a system of rights and duties. The erotic experience becomes a social or legal phenomenon. A wife is obligated
to have sex with her husband. It is her duty, and it is a
husband's right as a man. As de Beauvoir says, "Marriage is
obscene in principle in so far as it transforms into rights and
duties those mutual relations which should be founded on a spontaneous urge...."[25] The difference between love and duty is
clear: The former is freely performed out of spontaneous desire
or inclination and cannot be commanded, while duty, on the other
hand, is an act performed out of obligation. She claims that
sexual relations which are not performed out of true spontaneous
desire, as well as concern for the other, tend to degenerate into
a kind of "joint masturbation."[26]

However, one might argue that a woman is always free to
deny her husband sexual relations if she really desires to do so.
She can choose not to do her duty. But the problem here is that
a woman cannot really choose to break the contract unless she is
willing to live independently of her husband. But if she
actually makes this choice, if she says, "I no longer sexually
desire you, nor do I love you," the consequences for her are
extremely severe. That is simply because the ordinary housewife
has no independent means of support. She is economically dependent upon her husband. Divorce would be punishment akin to
imprisonment and dispossession. Thus even though theoretically
she may have the choice to break the contract, given her financial

situation, coupled with her lack of training and experience in the job market, to make such a choice would have dire consequences both for her and for her children, if she has any. As de Beauvoir says, "Divorce is only a theoretical possibility for the woman who cannot earn her own living."[27] Hence in such a relationship, sexual relations take on the form of a contractual agreement much like the relation between a prostitute and her client.[28] The man provides financial support in return for sexual favors from his wife. The only significant difference is the length of the contract. Whether there is desire or love in the relationship is really not the question. One consequence of this situation of financial dependency is that mothers who understand the reality of marital relations often tell their daughters to forget about love and marry with an eye to such practical concerns as financial well-being.[29] Hence, if the child follows her mother's advice, the situation of marriage without love is perpetuated over and over again.

Being financially dependent upon her husband means that a woman is not equal to her husband. He is essential for her well-being and livelihood. Because she is dependent, she is not seen as his equal. But, as we have seen, de Beauvoir believes that equality is a necessary condition for friendship as she has defined it. Thus, the traditional marriage where a wife is economically dependent upon her husband is not only the enemy of

234

the erotic, but is also the enemy of friendship. If erotic
pleasure and friendship are essential elements of conjugal love,
then such dependency also destroys conjugal love. Hence, given
de Beauvoir's position, if healthy conjugal love is to exist
within the institution of marriage, a woman must achieve economic
independence.

However, there are still problems. No matter how much
freedom economic independence allows a woman in terms of her sexual
relationship to her husband, it does not follow without further
qualification that such independence will lead to the experience
of erotic pleasure. Economic independence in itself only means
that the woman now has a choice, without suffering dire economic
consequences, whether or not to submit to her husband's sexual
advances. However, such economic independence does not entail
that each will in fact desire the other. But it does seem that
such independence could have positive effects upon her desire
for her husband and the husband's desire for her. This needs to
be examined.

De Beauvoir has emphasized throughout her description of
woman's oppression that labor is the key to self-development,
that one becomes what one is through labor. If the person does
nothing, the person is nothing. Given this perspective, it seems
reasonable to say that if a wife becomes involved in meaningful
labor outside of the home, she may then develop not only financial
independence, but realize her own potentials as a human being.

Through her labor outside of the home, a wife may become an individual quite apart from her relation to her husband. Rather than
living vicariously through her husband, she may attain recognition
and a social identity quite apart from him.[30]

But how in particular might this social recognition affect
their erotic relationship? Through her labor in the world she
attains an integrity and sense of herself independent of her
husband. These are important elements of erotic love as de
Beauvoir understands it. Whenever she describes ideal human
relations, the notions of individual integrity, freedom, and
reciprocity are always included. In her chapter on sexual initiation she says that the problem of sexuality

> ...can be easily solved when woman finds in the
> male both desire and respect; if he lusts after
> her flesh while recognizing her freedom, she
> feels herself essential, her integrity remains
> unimpaired...she remains free in the submission
> to which she consents...under a concrete and
> carnal form there is mutual recognition....[31]

Such respect and freedom are realized only through a wife's
ability to be a person quite apart from her husband. In her
chapter on the married woman she says, love is "a free assumption
of desire and pleasure,...but this is possible only when the
other is recognized as an individual."[32] But such individuality,
according to de Beauvoir, comes only from being engaged in
meaningful labor. Labor allows a woman to transcend the unhealthy
dependency of the traditional relationship towards de Beauvoir's
ideal.

> Some mates are united by a strong sexual love that
> leaves them free in their friendships and in their
> work; others are held together by a friendship
> that does not preclude sexual liberty; more rare
> are those who are at once lovers and friends <u>but
> do not seek in each other their sole reason for
> living</u>.[33] (emphasis mine)

The key to being "at once lovers and friends" is not only
economic equality, but the equality of mutual self-respect because
each <u>is</u> equally fulfilled as a person quite apart from the
marital relation. A man cannot merely grant his wife equality.
In such a situation, he, as the bestower of equality, remains
superior. The needed equality is achieved only through work.[34]
If love is indeed "a free exchange between equals," the partners
must in reality be equal.[35] If one remains dependent, that one
must always accept the will of the other.

Hence, a case can be made that the problem of marriage
reducing sex to a woman's duty and killing the erotic pleasure can
be solved to a great extent through economic equality and subsequently the woman developing her own self-concept and personhood
through labor in the world.

However, according to de Beauvoir, there is another problem
which undermines the experience of erotic pleasure in marriage.
In some places de Beauvoir contends that the truly erotic
experience depends upon the otherness of the other. The erotic
is a kind of sexual adventure into the unknown.[36] However, the
nature of repeated sexual encounters with the same person seems
to contradict this aspect of the erotic. She has argued that it

is absolute absurdity to believe that one person can meet the sexual needs of another for an entire lifetime.[37] Can this problem also be overcome through a woman engaging in meaningful labor?

Such a question may well be merely an empirical one. Whether or not one person can or cannot fulfill another's sexual needs over an extended period of time surely is a question to be answered in each individual case. However, one might argue that if love is an art, one improves one's techniques with practice. This idea is implied in de Beauvoir's description of the failure which accompanies the normal marriage night. The major problem with the "first night experience" is typically a lack of skill on the part of partners. If love is an art, one's performance should be enhanced with experience. On the other hand, Frederick Elliston, argues in his essay, "In Defense of Promiscuity," that one's skills as a lover will increase greatly through sexual encounters with many lovers, not through remaining in a monogamous relationship.[38]

In any case, one could argue that the likelihood of a life-long sexually satisfying relationship would at least be more likely if a woman is more than a mere slave to a man. If a woman's self-identity were continually growing and changing, she would be a more able adversary in "the battle of the sexes," a more interesting opponent. She would not be "mere clay in the man's hands," which from de Beauvoir's perspective is an enemy of any erotic experience. And finally, such personal growth might also mean that not as much emphasis need be placed on sexual relations. A married woman would not see being a sex object as her fundamental reason for living. If, on the other hand, the only thing interesting about a woman is her sexuality, and in the course of performing her marital duties this becomes commonplace, the relationship is reduced to one of boredom.

But, if a woman becomes more interesting through engaging in meaningful labor, the partners may have something to talk about on those long winter evenings. Rather than being for all practical purposes the man's sexual slave, the woman might achieve the level of being a _friend_ in the highest sense of that word: one who through a critical stance aids the personal development of her mate.[39] Such a relationship would be the antithesis of the typical husband-wife relation which de Beauvoir describes so poignantly.

> They live side by side without too much mental
> torment, too much lying to each other. But there
> is one curse they seldom escape: it is boredom.
> Whether the husband succeeds in making his wife an
> echo of himself or each is entrenched within a
> private universe, after some months or years they
> have nothing left to say to each other...they are
> statically united, they are "one" instead of
> maintaining a dynamic and living relation. This
> is the reason why they can give each other nothing,
> exchange nothing, whether in the realm of ideas
> or the erotic plane.[40]

On the other hand, in her ideal relationship each person is a free independent being. "The ideal on the contrary would be for entirely self-sufficient human beings to form unions one with another only in accordance with the untrammeled dictates of mutual love."[41] The key here is <u>self-sufficiency</u>. Being self-sufficient, a woman's love is no longer the mere acceptance of her plight or the expression of her weakness in terms of financial need.

However, if labor entails personal growth, it is entirely possible that each may grow apart from the other. But even if this occurs, at least the wife, being no longer financially dependent, has the option of ending the relationship and seeking her happiness elsewhere.

A woman's independence would also mean that her husband would no longer have the feeling of taking care of his "little woman," that feeling of false superiority sometimes confused with love. And of course, a woman's independence would mean that she would no longer look at her husband as the "great protector and provider." But this "sick" sort of dependence would be replaced by a dynamic relation between self-sufficient beings, each giving to the other out of strength and overflowing rather than parasitically living off the other out of weakness.

Before moving on to examine the apparent difficulties with respect to loving congenial relations which arise from de Beauvoir's ontology, there is yet another practical concern which needs to be discussed. We have seen that an argument can be made that fulfilling human relations within marriage are possible only if both the man and the woman are free, self-sufficient, equal

240

human beings. The means to such freedom and equality for women is through labor; not just any labor, but that which is equal in quality and pay to a man's.

This is all very clear. But the problem is, how will women become such persons through their labor if, first, there are not the opportunities present in the work world, and secondly women have been socialized to feel perfectly content being housewives, mothers, and generally second-class citizens? Since their infancies, women have been taught that they should feel at home living the life of the mother/housekeeper. How can this attitude be altered? How can women achieve equal power through equal opportunity if, because of their willingness to endorse the traditional sex-roles, they will not band together to struggle for the needed social changes? Hence it would seem that the needed social changes in terms of equal opportunity and equal pay are dependent on a radical change in attitude by women. But the change in attitude is unlikely to occur as long as women are taught to believe that motherhood is a sacred duty, that being a domestic worker is an acceptable goal, and that the passive doll-like feminine behaviors are more fitting for a woman than rationality and assertiveness. Not only are women educated along these lines, many wholeheartedly believe that they benefit from these roles.[42] This is why according to de Beauvoir, so many women are unwilling to fight against the conservative attitude which perpetuates the status quo.[43] The situation is analogous to the "false consciousness" of many workers, who, according to Marx, believe

that capitalism is really in their best interests and hence

refuse to join labor unions or socialist parties. As de Beauvoir

says in the conclusion to The Second Sex,

> We have seen that all the main features of her
> training combine to bar her from the roads of
> revolt and adventure. Society in general,
> beginning with her respected parents, lies to
> her by praising the lofty values of love, devotion,
> the gift of herself...she cheerfully believes
> these lies because they invite her to follow the
> easy slope...If a child is taught idleness by
> being amused all day long and never being led to
> study, or shown its usefulness, it will hardly be
> said when he grows up, that he chose to be incapable
> and ignorant; yet this is how woman is brought up,
> without ever being impressed with the necessity of
> taking charge of her own existence. So she
> readily lets herself come to count on the pro-
> tection, love, assistance, and supervision of
> others, she lets herself be fascinated with the
> hope of self-realization without doing anything.[44]

In short, a kind of revolution in women's consciousness is

needed for women to attain the needed freedom and equality, but

women, because of their education and childhood training, are not

revolutionaries, nor are they ready to support those who are.

Thus, although de Beauvoir is clear on the evils of the status quo

and is brilliant in describing the causes of the injustices, in

the end we are left with the question, 'What can be done?' The

Second Sex appears to end on a pessimistic tone.

Yet one might ask, what about socialism? Isn't it a

possible answer? We have seen that in at least three places in

The Second Sex, de Beauvoir says that socialism is a necessary

condition of women's freedom and equality.[45] This is because in
a socialistic system all would be forced to work and the women
would be given jobs equal to men's, and be given equal pay and
provided with child care. Such equal work and pay would result
in equal power. Twenty-five years after the publishing of The
Second Sex, in an interview with Sartre, de Beauvoir reemphasized
her position that the women's movement was closely tied to the
emancipation of all oppressed classes through socialism, and that
efforts should be made to convince all women of this position.[46]
In another interview, she explained that socialism was a necessary,
although not a sufficient condition for the desired freedom and
equality. However, she said that women should continue to work
for feminist goals rather than join existing socialist movements.
This is because countries which presently call themselves
"socialist" have not really brought about the needed change in
women's situations. Furthermore, if a women's revolution
occurred, de Beauvoir believes that it would in itself do a good
deal to destroy capitalism.[47] This is because, "...if women really
did have complete equality with men, society would be completely
overturned. For instance, there is the problem of unpaid labor,
such as housework, which represents millions and millions of
unsalaried hours and on which the masculine society is firmly based.
To put an end to this would be to send the present-day capitalist
system flying in a single blow."[48]

However, if we believe what de Beauvoir says in The Second
Sex, creating such radical feminists is no easy task. To be
revolutionary, women would have to be educated to be like boys,
that is, to be rational, creative, and assertive, and above all
to realize that they are responsible for their own fate, that no
one is going to care for them. But to be educated as such already
presupposes a society with parents and an educational system which
are no longer sexist. If, on the other hand, "she is raised like
a boy" in our present sexist society, "the young girl feels an
oddity and thereby she is given a new kind of sex specification.
Stendhal understood this when he said, 'the forest must be planted
all at once!'"[49] Because the solution presupposes that the
problem is already solved, de Beauvoir seems to be suggesting
that the society must already be completely revolutionized before
the new revolutionary women can be created. Slow change is
impossible. Like Plato in his Republic, the ideal can only become
real if the slate, filled with all past injustices, is wiped
clean. The ideal society requires wise rulers, but wise rulers
only occur in ideal states with ideal educational systems.

In a 1976 interview, however, de Beauvoir appears much more
optimistic about the possibility of change. Although she says
that the psychological changes in women's attitudes needed for a
social change will be very difficult to attain, that a kind of
revolution is possible if certain steps are followed.

> First, such peoples (those economically and
> politically dominated) must become aware of
> that domination. Then they have to believe
> in their own strength to change it. Those
> who profit from the "collaboration" have to
> understand their betrayal. And finally, those
> who have the most to lose from taking a stand,
> that is women like me who have earned out a
> successful sinecure or career, have to be
> willing to risk insecurity...in order to gain
> self-respect.[50]

However, apart from the occurrence of these psychological conditions, she says there must be adequate technological development such that women can see that it is in their own interest, regardless of physical weakness, to engage in meaningful labor in the society. Equality for these individuals then becomes a real possibility. And ironically, if women were to attain this desired equality, de Beauvoir believes this would at the same time undermine the exploitive capitalistic system which depends on "such institutions as churches, marriage, armies, and the millions of factories, shops, stores, etc., which are dependent on piece work, part-time work, and cheap labor."[51]

There is a certain amount of an ironic dialectical inversion in this account of social change. On one hand de Beauvoir believes that even if the technological advances of society have made it possible for some women to attain equality, there would remain a great tendency for these women to be "feminists" simply because "they want a bigger piece of the pie. They want to earn more, elect more women to parliaments, see a woman become president. They fundamentally believe in inequality, except they

want to be on top rather than on bottom."[52]   But the fact that more
and more women do in fact enter the working world, no matter what
their political ideologies, or their motives, the greater the
chance that capitalism and its exploitive structure would collapse
and socialism take its place.[53]

Hence, in spite of the false consciousness present in most
women, de Beauvoir believes that women entering the working world
will aid the establishment of socialism. The needed revolutionary
consciousness is not really necessary because the system will
change in spite of the motives and intentions of women.

How does socialism solve the problem of women's equality?
De Beauvoir is not very clear on this issue in The Second Sex,
beyond the notion that all women should be forced to work and
that this in itself would greatly enhance their position in
becoming equals to men. In addition to this argument, there are
a number of other arguments that could be brought up.

First, it could be argued that socialism would do away
with the institution of private property. Private property is
essentially in men's hands. It is one important way that men have
maintained their power over women. It gives them economic
and political power. Economic supremacy leads to man's supremacy
in the family (the opposite of Aristotle's account). The woman
is dependent upon the man and is thus unequal. If the institution
of private property were abolished, much of the power that men
have which is built on that institution would be dissipated.[54]

One might also go on to argue that if private property were abolished, the tendency of a man to look at his wife as his property would also be diminished. Private property, as a basis for patriarchy, would be absent. New attitudes and relations besides owner/owned relations could then arise. No longer being "owned" and dependent, a woman could freely choose whether or not to enter into sexual relations with her husband.

De Beauvoir pointed out in her chapter on the "Independent Woman," that currently, because women tend to be given the poorer jobs and poorer wages, even if they do work they are still members of the most oppressed class -- the proletariat.[55] Socialism, by doing away with private property and hence the class structure based on that foundation, would place women on much more equal footing with their male fellow-workers. Even if women were paid less than men, at least they would no longer be the oppressed members of the oppressed class. They would simply be oppressed.

Given such arguments, a strong case can certainly be made that women would be better off in a socialist economy which forced them to work and hence escape their dependency upon men. The result of this would be better sexual relations with men and, as has already been pointed out, the women would be better mothers.[56] I find it very hard to argue against de Beauvoir's conclusion.

The claim that de Beauvoir makes that is not so clear is why "if all women work as much as men," this would in the end destroy capitalism.[57] As we have seen, she believes this is the case because women working would undermine institutions upon which capitalism depends: "churches, marriage, armies, and the millions of factories, shops, stores, etc., which are dependent on piece work, part-time work, and cheap labor."[58] Hence there are two claims. First, she is claiming that capitalism depends on certain institutions for its survival. And second, she is claiming that if all women worked like men, this would destroy these institutions and subsequently destroy capitalism.

These are important but problematic claims. There has already been a good deal of scholarly work trying to analyze the connections between the success of capitalism and the traditional family.[59] Generally, there is a shared belief among socialist feminists that, as de Beauvoir says, capitalism is grounded upon a basis of the unpaid labor of the housewife and the traditional institution of marriage.

Why the family is the foundation upon which capitalism rests is never exactly clear. That is not to say that there are not arguments given; it is that I simply have trouble understanding the logic of the arguments. And secondly, even if I do think I understand the arguments, I can always imagine possible states of affairs where women are working like men, the traditional family is non-existent, and yet, capitalism still survives.

For example, it has been argued that capitalism is dependent on the existence of the traditional family in so far as the family

248

teaches women and their children to be good consumers. Having no
life apart from consuming, or as de Beauvoir would say, no
outlet for their truly human energies, these women find themselves
in things. Housewives become the quintessential consumers for
capitalist products.[61] It is also argued that women in the traditional family also provide a potential work force which can be
exploited at a low wage if the capitalist is in need of laborers,
as was the case during World War I and World War II. When the
need is over, these women can be laid off and easily reabsorbed
into the society because they are supported by their husbands.[62]
Such women never considered to be 'really' employed. They are
merely housewives who have taken on extra work.

In response to such arguments I would first point out that
although the women who stay at home do tend to be excellent
consumers, it is my own experience that men who work (or women
for that matter) are not exactly ascetics who have taken vows of
poverty. Men too make excellent consumers. With reference to
children, it seems that they hardly need their mothers to teach
them to be consumers. They have television for that.

With respect to the second part of the above argument, that
women who are housewives provide the capitalist with a convenient
labor pool to exploit for low wages in times of need, I have but
a minor objection. It is generally accepted that capitalism
functions more smoothly (exploits more easily) when there is a pool
of unemployed workers. But I see no reason why these unemployed
workers must be women. If, as de Beauvoir wishes, all women work

and the opportunity to be nothing but a housewife/mother is non-existent, then the pool of workers will increase significantly and a certain percent of these will be unemployed because of the inevitable fluctuations in the market under capitalism. But as long as there is a pool of unemployed workers, I don't see why it is _necessary_ for capitalism that this pool be housewives. It is clearly _convenient,_ but not _necessary._ It seems to me that a pool of unemployed are unemployed, regardless of their sex.

One might contend that because of women's tendency to see being employed as the exception rather than the rule, that they more easily accept unemployment. The ease with which they accept such treatment makes capitalism run more smoothly. But it does not follow that the system would "self-destruct" if women expected to be employed just like men and were equally upset at being unemployed.

There is another argument given that the housewife's work is essential to capitalism because it provides necessary services for male workers, but is done for free.[63] The argument says that if it were not for this free labor, the male worker would have to hire all of his cooking, washing, cleaning, etc., done, and this would significantly raise the amount of money that he needs to live on, or as Marx would say, his "subsistence wage." If, because of this new expenditure, his wages were raised this would in turn mean that the cost of goods and services would have to be increased to cover the added costs in wages. Hence if women

250

worked _and_ at the same time refused to perform their duties as
"housekeepers," the system would be destroyed.

This argument is likewise problematic. It may be the case
that a man's wages can be kept down if a woman does a good deal of
his essential tasks free. But if a woman works for a wage away
from the home, this would mean that the family income would be
significantly increased and the family could hire someone else to
do a good deal of the household tasks previously done for free
by the woman; i.e., washing, ironing, cleaning, using fast-food
restaurants and microwave ovens, and child care. A woman's working
would actually create more "capitalization" of family activities.
It would create the demand for a new cadre of workers in these
service-oriented professions.

Unless there are further arguments, I believe one can
seriously question de Beauvoir's claim that if all women worked
like men, capitalism would be destroyed. While it can be shown
that capitalism benefits from the existence of various traditional
family-related institutions, it is not clear that these institutions are necessary conditions for its existence.

Thus to conclude this discussion, we have seen that de
Beauvoir believes the major problems with male-female sexual
relations can be overcome if there is a kind of freedom, equality,
and friendship between the two people. These conditions can best
be realized if a woman works and becomes self-sufficient. But
due to the "easy path" of choosing to be a housewife rather than

to engage upon a career, de Beauvoir feels that socialism is needed to "force women to be free." This is because, under her version of socialism, women would be forced to work in jobs like men. Finally, we saw that she believed that if women worked like men work, capitalism would fail because it is grounded on the certain traditional institutions. As we have just seen, this claim is very problematic.

IV. Ontological Problems and Human Relations

Apart from the difficulties of trying to work out political solutions to the problems of male-female relations within the framework of traditional marriage, I believe that there are problems which arise from de Beauvoir's ontology which in effect could appear to make practical solutions impossible. That is, to put it quite simply, her ontology concerning human nature makes love or friendship, as it is generally understood, impossible. We have seen that for de Beauvoir and other thinkers, spontaneous good will between humans is considered to be an essential part of love or friendship. However, her Sartrean ontology appears to preclude the possibility of such good-will.

We saw in chapter one that according to de Beauvoir, consciousness naturally seeks to dominate and oppress other consciousnesses. As she says in the introduction, "...we find in consciousness itself a fundamental hostility toward every other consciousness...."[64] And in the conclusion of the book, after

numerous other such statements,[65] she still holds the position
that the tendency to oppress others is natural to human consciousness.

> Oppression is to be explained by the tendency of
> the existent to flee from himself by means of
> identification with the other, whom he oppresses
> to that end. In each man that tendency exists
> today....The husband wants to find himself in
> his wife, the lover in his mistress, in the form
> of a stone image; he is seeking in her the myth
> of his virility, of his sovereignty, of his
> immediate reality.[66]

In this important passage, it is apparent that de Beauvoir
has adopted the Sartrean ontology that was described in chapter
one of this work. As we have seen, for Sartre consciousness seeks
to find itself through the recognition of other consciousnesses.
The oppression that follows is a result of consciousness' attempt
to force the other to recognize it. From this perspective, love
is but a masked or subtle attempt of consciousness to _force_ the
other to _freely_ recognize it as a sovereign, essential being.
Love is then yet another attempt of consciousness to become God,
to take on an identity of a free, necessary, essential being who
does not need to justify its existence. It is but a veiled
attempt by consciousness to oppress the other.[67] Any notion of
love which includes the idea of genuine care and concern would
be a misunderstanding of consciousness' fundamental project.

Yet, while de Beauvoir subscribes to the Sartrean ontology,
it does not appear that she holds the position that love as

genuine mutual recognition is impossible. In the conclusion of
the book, as well as in numerous other places, she talks about
the possibility of an ideal reciprocal relation between the
sexes with each "mutually recognizing the other as subject...."[68]
There is some question as to just what she means. It is possible
that to mutually recognize the other as a subject may mean that
each chooses to give up his or her fundamental project of oppressing
the other. In order to be consistent, she could not mean that each
gives recognition to the other out of genuine "amorous inclinations." That is precluded on ontological grounds. In fact, she
does say that regardless of the tendency for each person to seek
to oppress the other, it is possible for human beings not to act
on those tendencies.[69] Such congenial behavior would at least
create the appearance of a loving relationship.

However, our analysis of her notion of love brought out
that she included an emotional element such that the person in
love genuinely desired the well-being of the loved one. How can
this emotional feeling of good-will be explained if we accept
what she says about human nature? From the perspective of
Sartrean ontology, for one to give the appearance of genuine concern should be understood simply as one more attempt of one to
dominate the other; that is, one behaves as if one loves the other
person in order to control the other person.

Being able to choose to act as if one felt concern for the
other is clearly not the same as acting with the genuine feeling

of good will towards another person. This was Sartre's position
when he pointed out in <u>Being and Nothingness</u> that love as a
desire is distinct from freely choosing to act affectionately
towards another.[70] Hence, even if de Beauvoir allows that
human freedom can overcome the tendency to oppress others, her
ontology still precludes the possibility of the needed emotional
elements of love: good will, care, and genuine affection.

One possible way out of the apparent impasse would be if
de Beauvoir held the position that although at the present time
humans are in fact always inclined to oppress others, that such a
tendency is really but a product of the society in which humans
find themselves. And if this society were altered, so too would
the tendency to oppress. That she would be sympathetic to such
a suggestion is given some support in her critique of the biological explanation of feminine behavior. As we have seen, she
is critical of any view of human nature which sees humans as
having a fixed nature.[71] She says that while animals have fixed
essences and it is hence possible to define them in static terms,
"the human species is forever in a state of change, forever
becoming."[72] The changes in human nature that occur are due to
the fact that humans always interact with an environment which
itself is always changing because of the effects of human labor.
As the environment has changed, new possibilities would be
created, and new human dispositions would be developed in response
to these possibilities. Given this rather Marxian position, what

now appears to be 'human nature' could be radically changed if the society were changed. Antagonism might be replaced with heart-felt benevolence.

If we were to apply this sort of interpretation of de Beauvoir's ontology to the realm of sexual relations in marriage some important consequences might follow. If the society were altered such that women were engaged in socially meaningful labor, their development would lead to power equal to the power men have in the traditional society. If women were in fact equal to men and perceived as such, then the oppression which results from inequality might be overcome. Because of these real changes, the attitudes towards women would also change. Through such equality the mutual respect that de Beauvoir sees as necessary for love might finally manifest itself. Love, as genuine care for the well-being of the other, would be possible.

This sort of analysis if another way of saying that attitudes or human dispositions will truly change only when, as Marx says, the material conditions change. This also appears to be de Beauvoir's position in The Force of Circumstance where she claims that if she were to rewrite The Second Sex she would "take a more materialistic position."[73] Additional evidence that de Beauvoir would support such an interpretation is given in her continual appeal to the virtues of socialism as the means to overcoming women's oppression.[74]

However, if one believes that de Beauvoir is committed to the Sartrean ontology of Being and Nothingness, the problem of giving a plausible account of love still remains. Be that as it may, I believe that such an account can be constructed which is not only consistent with what she says in The Second Sex but raises love above the typical romantic ideal which de Beauvoir believes does so much to enslave both men and women. I believe that an account can be given based on the idea that love involves a kind of struggle, but that the struggle is a healthy one.

First it should be remembered that de Beauvoir believes that when two people 'love' each other that they can rise above the tendency openly to oppress each other. This can occur when the persons have a shared concern for some external goal and each perceives the other as a means to attaining that goal. Her analysis of marriage clearly exemplifies this notion. She has pointed out that a woman typically gets married because she perceives that her goals (security, social acceptance, and sexual pleasure) can best be achieved through a marital relation with a certain man. A man typically shares many of these same goals and sees his marriage to the woman as a means to attaining these goals. Hence each person sees the other as a means to attaining his or her ideals. Because of this it could be said that each genuinely likes, values, and shows concern for the other. In such a, situation the project of becoming 'a typical middle-class family' may take precedence of the natural tendency of each to oppress the other. Thus, each would at least behave as if each loved the other simply for prudential reasons.

Or, to use another example, if both members of the marriage simply desire sexual pleasure, and each perceives the other as a means to that end, the desire to oppress the other might not be acted upon, at least while each satisfied the other's sexual desires.

Unfortunately, if taken by itself, such an analysis of love is rather shallow. It is an example of what Aristotle called the lowest form of friendship, a relation based totally on utility. As soon as the goal is achieved or something happens that the people believe that the goal is no longer attainable, the relation also ceases. This example is analogous to Sartre's example of the group of revolutionaries storming the Bastille. They all have a common goal and are hence colleagues. But once the goal is attained they again become individuals, each by nature seeking to oppress the other.[75] This tendency is controlled when the group, no longer united by a common goal, sets up a constitution of laws to unite the individuals and to protect the rights of the individual. Lacking shared immediate objectives, the group remains intact through defining long-term objectives or as in the case of political parties, a constitution stating long-term political goals. But there is no "love" or concern for the other.

The irony according to Sartre's analysis is that the group
initially formed because they shared a common goal. The attainment
of the goal was to give them more freedom as individuals. But
once the goal was attained, the group, in order to continue to
exist, formed a Party or Constitution which had the effect of
limiting the freedom of the individuals. In the same sense, for
de Beauvoir, if we saw the union of two people in marriage as an
attempt to achieve some common goals which would allow each
person more pleasure and freedom, once the goals were attained
or their attainment was judged impossible, the purpose of the
marital relation would dissolve. Unfortunately, the marriage
itself is not so easily dissolved; the institution, as all
institutions, tends to outlive its usefulness. In this respect,
the institution destroys the freedom of the individuals who
initially entered into the relationship in order to attain
greater freedom. When this situation occurs, the natural antagonism between the respective consciousnesses is reestablished,
and because the woman is the dependent member of the relationship, she is the one who is typically exploited.

However, one thing that this sort of analysis of love does
is to redefine and in some sense 'demystify' the traditional
notion of romantic love. There are accounts, such as that
given by Sharon Bishop in her essay, "Love and Dependency,"[76]
which emphasize the uniqueness of the beloved and hold that love
is to be understood as something over and above simply seeing

the other as a means to satisfying social, emotional, and physical desires. Intuitively, such accounts have their appeal; that is, most of us like to think that we are loved for reasons over and above the services we provide. However, I believe that when one begins questioning the nature of the unique quality which inspires the love and devotion of another person, it becomes very difficult to say what it is over and above the ability to provide 'the pleasant and the useful' to the other person.

An interesting thought experiment which will help illustrate my point is to list all of the attributes of the person one loves and then ask if all of those qualities were altered would one continue to 'love' the person. For example, if some of the attributes of the loved one included that person's ability to provide financial support, stimulating companionship, and sexual pleasure, would one still love that person if all or even some of these qualities were destroyed? Another interesting question would be to ask, once the list of attributes was compiled, would another person with all or most of these qualities serve just as well as a mate?

Those who argue for the unique nature of love, over and above the beloved's abilities to satisfy one's desires, would have to say that even if the person lost the ability to provide financial support, to provide stimulating companionship, and to provide sexual pleasure, the person would still be loved for that "unique something" which raises love above relations merely based on utility. Love, as Shakespeare once said, "alters not when it alteration finds."

I believe that it is this kind of thinking, perhaps grounded in the Christian belief in the value and uniqueness of each individual soul, which has created a good deal of pain and suffering in this world. It is the kind of thinking which underlies the traditional marriage vows which include the pledge to love the other no matter what happens, 'til death do us part.' In this tradition even if the person no longer provides the 'useful and the agreeable', that person is supposed to be loved. (This is the same tradition that sees suffering as a virtue.)

I believe that a case can be made that if there is a unique quality in a relationship, that it is the sharing of a common history which only two people who have lived together for many years can experience. As the years go by, the person may become unique when one recognizes that this is the only other person on earth with whom one can discuss one's past and who understands the significance of certain personal events. If this is true, that uniqueness should grow with time. Of course if the history is, as de Beauvoir claims, full of boredom and mediocrity stretched over endless days and nights, this unique shared experience would hardly be an asset.

With the emphasis that de Beauvoir places on utility, the mysterious element of youthful romantic love is reduced to pragmatic terms. Simply put, people enter into relationships primarily because they perceive that they can more easily satisfy their desires and attain their goals with the help of the other who shares these desires: a very Hobbesian picture. When it becomes apparent that the person no longer is effective in attaining these goals, "consciousness's natural hostility towards other consciousnesses" again raises its ugly head.

In order to complete this interpretation of de Beauvoir's analysis of love, let us move beyond the simple concerns of physical, emotional, and social usefulness. Simple utility is not the whole story. As previously mentioned, I believe that one can argue that under certain conditions the continual struggle between a man and a wife could be a healthy relationship. However, the condition for such a healthy relation must be that each of the persons has equal power. If each were equal, neither could oppress the other. That is to say, even if one adopts the Sartrean model where consciousness is always trying to oppress the other, the oppression of one person by another could not occur unless there was an unequal distribution of power. Thus man may naturally oppress woman as long as he has an excess of power which allows him to dominate her. But, as de Beauvoir says, if both are able to resist this position, "there is created between them a reciprocal relation...If one of the two is in some way privileged, has some advantage, this one prevails over the other and undertakes to keep it in subjection."[77] Hence only if there is in fact equal power can the effects of the fundamental hostility

of every consciousness towards other consciousnesses be nullified.
What results is a kind of dynamic, and hopefully healthy, tension
between the two people who are mutually attracted to each other
for utilitarian and sexual reasons, rather than blatant subjuga-
tion and oppression.[78]

From this perspective, one might suppose, in a sort of
Nietzschean fashion, that each member of such a relation would
perceive that through the struggle for recognition each was made
psychologically stronger and hence better. If this happened each
would see how important the other was in his or her own development as a human being and perhaps "love" the other. Each would
perceive the value of the dialectical relation where each makes
the other a better person, a kind of Socratic relation.

That such a notion is close to de Beauvoir's is evident
when she says, "An individual who is loved as a free being, in
his humanity, is regarded with that critical demanding severity
which is the other side of genuine esteem."[79] She sounds almost
as if she has the Nietzschean ideal in mind where one's greatest
friend is one's greatest enemy. As Nietzsche says, "In your
friend you should possess your best enemy...Are you a slave?
If so, you cannot be a friend."[80] Such an interpretation is given
further credence by the fact that she is critical of women who
offer "unconditional devotion" to their husbands because it harms
both the woman and the man.[81] Such love benefits neither; it
lacks the critical severity that only two persons who are both free

and equal can give to each other, a severity which forces each to grow through its relentless questioning. If both members are free and equal, then the attempt of each to oppress the other and gain recognition will be the occasion for each to become better and stronger in order to deserve the recognition. Each grows in the other's presence. If both recognize this, then it may be the case that each feels a genuine care and concern for the other because each sees that each becomes what he or she becomes through the dialectical relation to the other.

If we accept these interpretations, what de Beauvoir has in effect done is to redefine conjugal love in terms of the Nietzschean or Greek notion of friendship, rather than the romantic idea prevalent in modern society. To love is not to look for someone to worship, but for a worthy opponent with whom to do battle and who may be of help in satisfying one's desires. This sort of relationship would completely undermine the romantic ideal which, as we have seen, de Beauvoir believes does so much to enslave women by forcing them to play the role of sex objects rather than developing the skills necessary to get along well in the world.

The traditional notion of romantic love sees the relations between a man and a woman as affairs of the heart where the other is seen as some sort of ideal. The woman is seen as the ideal of changeless beauty, while the man is seen as Prince Charming. As we have seen, both of these roles destroy the equality and

freedom needed for what de Beauvoir believes are ideal relationships.

Whether or not in de Beauvoir's scheme there is any emotional
feeling toward the other, over and above seeing that the other is
sexually desirable and a worthy intellectual adversary, is an
interesting question. Perhaps it is enough to say that love is
really nothing but sexual desire and enlightened self-interest,
where we are emotionally drawn to the other because we see that
the other can aid us in the development of our higher potentials,
aid us in achieving our practical goals and projects, and can
satisfy us sexually. Perhaps when these conditions are present
then the "heart" likewise has its emotional response. While
traditional romantic love placed the emphasis on the "heart"
first and the more practical concerns later, one can see that de
Beauvoir, while including the emotional element, has reversed
the order of importance. In doing this, she has made it possible
for conjugal love, as newly defined, to lead to the health and
freedom of each person, even though consciousness is always
disposed to subjugate the other.

V. Summary and Conclusion

We have seen that for de Beauvoir the sexual problems confronting married persons can be divided into two kinds. First,
there are those related specifically to the traditional institution
of marriage and the traditional roles alloted to women. We have

seen that a strong case can be made that the solution to these problems lies in changing the structures of the society, such that women are forced to work and through their labor become more or less equal to men. Such equality would allow women freely to relate to their husbands and it would also allow women to become more interesting as persons. Sexual relations between two equals would be more enjoyable than the master-slave relationship so often present in the traditional marriage.

Secondly, we saw that regardless of all social changes, de Beauvoir's ontology which portrays human consciousnesses as innately seeking to subjugate and oppress others, seems to preclude the possibility of two persons ever truly caring about each other. However, we saw that a case could be made that if each person were equal in power, the conflict between man and wife could be beneficial to both persons in terms of their personal growth. As beneficial each would perceive that the other was in his or her own best interest and genuinely "like" the other. This sort of analysis totally redefines the notion of "romantic love" and replaces it with a notion close to Socratic or Nietzschean friendship, coupled with erotic desire and self-interest. It was argued that each could perceive that the other whom one seeks to oppress, if a formidable opponent, actually is beneficial in terms of making one stronger and better.

It was also argued that this tendency to oppress others might not be innate and that de Beauvoir may believe that if one could change the social conditions one could change "human nature." That is one reason why she holds that socialism is necessary for women's liberation, and is her position some years after the writing of The Second Sex.

My position is that it makes more sense to argue that regardless of whether the human tendency to exploit and oppress others can be altered by restructuring society, if the problems which such a tendency creates can be nullified, the question is moot. Hence, even if people are always trying to oppress others, if all have relatively the same power, then no one class will be able to oppress others. If, as de Beauvoir suggests, women are forced to work at the same kinds of jobs as men and are paid equally, then they will have the power necessary to resist oppression. Under such conditions, the struggle between human consciousness may be a healthy dialectic where each grows through the other's presence.

I believe that de Beauvoir is quite right when she says that in order to attain such equality women must be raised like men, and the possibility of a woman choosing to be only a housewife/ mother must be negated. An equal opportunity to work at the jobs men work at is senseless without raising women so that they acquire the human skills necessary to compete with men in the working world. Women must be taught to be competitive, aggressive, and rational, rather than passive, coquettish, and emotional. In the business world some skills are clearly more effective than others, while in the world of romance other skills may be more effective. De Beauvoir is quite right when she points out that the "feminine virtues" have been developed so that women could excel in the world of romance, with marriage and motherhood as the goals. But she also has shown that these goals, once attained, destroy a woman's self development and enslave her. If woman wants to be free, she must be equal. If she is to become equal, she must attain equal power. In order to attain equal power, she must be able to be economically independent. However, in order to attain such independence, she must be able to compete with men in the man's world. To do this, she must develop the necessary "masculine virtues": rationality, self-control, aggressiveness, and self-transcendence.

If de Beauvoir's ontology is correct, that humans naturally are disposed to dominate others, and if women can develop these "masculine virtues" along with repertoires of "feminine virtues," I believe that not only will women be equal to men, but they will become even more powerful in the economic struggle for power. This is because their feminine attributes will allow them to manipulate the traditional "unsuspecting male" and their rational attributes will allow them to compete with these men who see them simply as peers.

But as de Beauvoir says, women will not seriously attempt to develop the needed masculine virtues until the opportunity of simply "being a housewife" is not afforded. Necessity may well be

268

the mother of invention, and until women have to compete with
men in order to survive, they will not develop the capacities
necessary for such competition.

FOOTNOTES

[1]SS 420, 481.

[2]SS 212, 498, 527, 534-535.

[3]That such a definition also coincides with many modern ideas concerning conjugal love is evident. See, Lyla H. O'Driscoll, "On the Nature and Value of Marriage," Feminism and Philosophy, eds. Mary Vetterling-Braggen, Frederick Elliston, and Jane English (Totowa, N.S.: Littlefield Adams, 1977), pp. 249-263. O'Driscoll emphasizes the notion that marital love entails both friendship in Aristotle's highest sense and affection of the erotic sort, while the former is the most important because one can have erotic affection for many persons, but not love many. See also Michael D. Bayles, "Marriage, Love and Procreation," in Philosophy and Sex, eds. Robert Baker and Frederick Elliston (Buffalo, N.Y.: Prometheus Books, 1975), pp. 140-206. Bayles also believes that sexual affection must be combined with "genuine concern" for the other's well-being before one can have an adequate notion of conjugal love. Sexual intercourse becomes truly significant only when performed with a person who is one's friend. One of the more careful accounts of ideal love between persons is given in Sharon Bishop's "Love and Dependency," Philosophy and Women, pp. 147-154. Bishop argues that love is a sentiment which is directed towards a unique person and which seeks the well-being of that person for the person's sake.

[4]It is uncanny that nearly all accounts of friendship are built on Aristotle's account in Bks. VIII and IX of his Nichomachean Ethics. Whether this is because the Western traditions have been deeply influenced by Aristotle or whether it is because what Aristotle had to say about friendship was true, I can only guess. I would guess that it is the latter.

[5]Aristotle, Nichomachean Ethics, Bk VIII, Ch. 5, 1157b, 35.

[6]Ibid., Ch. 6, 1158b.

[7]Ibid., Bk. VIII, Ch. 5, 1157b.

[8]Ibid., Bk. VIII, Ch. 3, 1156a.

[9]Ibid.

[10] _Ibid._

[11] _SS_ 687.

[12] _SS_ 774.

[13] _SS_ 484.

[14] _SS_ 619.

[15] _SS_ 211-212, 491, 498, 742, to name a few.

[16] Alan Goldman, "Plain Sex," _Philosophy and Public Affairs,_ Spring 1977, Vol. 6, #3, p. 268.

[17] _SS_ 491.

[18] _SS_ 492.

[19] _Ibid._

[20] _SS_ 528.

[21] _SS_ 528-529.

[22] _SS_ 528, see also Sharon Bishop's discussion in her "Love and Dependency," _op._ _cit_.

[23] _SS_ 527.

[24] _SS_ 212, 769.

[25] _SS_ 498.

[26] _Ibid._

[27] _SS_ 537.

[28] _SS_ 481.

^{29}SS 484.

^{30}Of course such optimism presupposes that the woman's labor
is not equally as stultifying as housework and it ignores the
problem of how a woman with so little practical training is
going to find a decent job. This also presupposes that the
husband will not resent his wife's new found freedom and his loss
of control over her.

^{31}SS 448.

^{32}SS 492.

^{33}SS 535-536.

^{34}SS 536.

^{35}SS 769.

^{36}SS 208, 211-212.

^{37}SS 497.

^{38}Frederick Elliston, "In Defense of Promiscuity," In
Philosophy and Sex, pp. 236-237.

^{39}SS 687.

^{40}SS 526-527.

^{41}SS 528.

^{42}SS XXIV.

^{43}Ibid.

^{44}SS 802.

^{45}SS 61, 123, 756.

[46] Jean-Paul Sartre, "Simone de Beauvoir Interviews Sartre," Life Situations (New York: Pantheon Books, 1977), pp. 93-108.

[47] Alice Jardine, "Interview with Simone de Beauvoir," Signs, 1979, Vol. 5, No. 2, pp. 224-236.

[48] Ibid., p. 227.

[49] SS 807.

[50] John Gerassi, "Simone de Beauvoir: The Second Sex 25 Years Later," Society, Jan/Feb. 1976, p. 80.

[51] Ibid.

[52] Ibid.

[53] This idea is also shared by George Gilder, in his book, Wealth and Poverty (New York: Basic Books, 1981), pp. 14-16. According to Gilder, not only does the working woman destroy the family and the values necessary for a good (productive) capitalistic economy, but women simply are not as productive as men and yet demand equal pay. Hence, they undercut the profits and productivity of the company, and endanger our nation's economic security.

[54] See Mihailo Markovic, "Women's Liberation and Human Emancipation," Philosophical Forum, Boston, 5, Fall-Winter, 1973, pp. 145-167.

[55] SS 756.

[56] SS 586.

[57] John Gerassi, op. cit., p. 80.

[58] Ibid.

[59] See Ann Foreman, Feminity as Alienation (London: Pluto Press, 1977). See especially Ch. 12 and her discussion of the literature; see also Eli Zaretsky, Capitalism: The Family and Personal Life (New York: Harper and Row, 1976).

[60] See Giuliana Pompei's article, "Wages for Housework," Feminist Frameworks, eds. Alison Jaggar and Paula Rothenberg Struhl (New York: McGraw-Hill, 1978), pp. 208-211. "Inside the home, we saw our invisible work, the enormous quantity of work that women are forced to perform each day in order to produce... the labour force, the invisible -because unpaid- foundation upon which the whole pyramid of capitalism rests." (p. 208)

[61] Margaret Benston, "The Political Economy of Women's Liberation," Feminist Frameworks, pp. 188-196.

[62] Ibid., pp. 193-194.

[63] Ibid., p. 195; see also "Socialist Feminism," by the staff of Women, in Feminist Frameworks, p. 207; and again, "Wages for Housework," by Guiliana Pompei, in Feminist Frameworks, p. 209.

[64] SS XX.

[65] See SS 64, 69, 151.

[66] SS 800.

[67] BN 367.

[68] SS 813. See also 769, 486, 492, 527-28.

[69] SS 800.

[70] BN 367.

[71] SS 37.

[72] Ibid.

[73] de Beauvoir, The Force of Circumstance, p. 192.

[74] SS 61, 123, 756.

[75] Sartre, Critique of Dialectical Reason, pp. 351-404.

[76]Sharon Bishop, "Love and Dependency," p. 149.

[77]SS 69.

[78]This sort of argument is the initial premise for the separatist's position that, in the current situation, the only solution to oppression is for women to separate themselves from the male dominated society. They too hold that liberation requires truly equal power, but that there can be no real equality in a society controlled by men. Hence, no healthy relations can occur between man and woman. For a man to grant a woman equal power is still for him to remain in a place of dominance like a God granting mankind forgiveness. See "Separation and Sexual Relation," Sara Ann Ketchum and Christine Pierce, in Philosophy and Women, pp. 167-171.

[79]SS 687.

[80]Friedrich Nietzsche, Thus Spoke Zarathustra, p. 83.

[81]SS 742.

BIBLIOGRAPHY

Anderson, Thomas C. "Is a Sartrean Ethics Possible?" Philosophy Today, Vol. 14, (1970), pp. 116-140.

_____. The Foundation and Structure of Sartrean Ethics. Lawrence, Ks.: Regents Press of Kansas, 1979.

Aristotle, The Basic Works of Aristotle. Ed. Richard McKeon. New York: Random House, 1941.

_____. Historia Animalium. In Women in Western Thought. Ed. Martha Lee Osborne. New York: Random House, 1979, pp. 36-37.

Badinter, Elizabeth. Mother Love: Myth and Reality. New York: Macmillan, 1980.

Barnes, Hazel. An Existentialist Ethics. Chicago: University of Chicago Press, 1968.

Barrett, William. Irrational Man. Garden City: Doubleday Anchor, 1962.

Beauvoir, Simone de. All Said and Done. Trans. Patrick O'Brian. New York: Putnam, 1974.

_____. The Coming of Age. Trans. Patrick O'Brian. New York: Putnam, 1972.

_____. The Ethics of Ambiguity. Trans. Bernard Gretchman. Secaucus, N.J.: Citadel Press, 1949.

_____. Force of Circumstance. Trans. Richard Howard. New York: Putnam, 1965.

_____. The Prime of Life. Trans. Peter Green. Cleveland: World, 1962.

_____. The Second Sex. Trans. H.M. Parshley. New York: Vintage, 1974.

Beiber, Konrad. Simone de Beauvoir. Boston: Twayne Publishing, 1979.

Benjamin, Jessica and Margaret Simons. "Simone de Beauvoir: An Interview." Feminine Studies, 5, Summer, 1979, pp. 330-345.

Benston, Margaret. "The Political Economy of Women's Liberation." Feminist Frameworks. Eds. Alison Jaggar and Paula Rothenberg-Struhl. New York: McGraw-Hill, 1978, pp. 188-196.

Berstein, Richard. Praxis and Action. Philadelphia: University of Pennsylvania Press, 1971.

Bishop, Sharon. "Love and Dependency." Philosophy and Women. Eds. Sharon Bishop and Marjorie Weinzweig. Belmont: Wadsworth, 1979, pp. 147-159.

Branden, Nathaniel. The Psychology of Romantic Love. Trans. John Jay Parry. New York: Ungar Publishing, 1957.

Caws, Peter. Sartre. Boston: Routledge & Kegan, 1979.

Collins, Margery and Christine Pierce. "Holes and Slime: Sexism in Sartre's Psychoanalysis." Philosophical Forum, 5, Boston, Fall-Winter, 1973, pp. 112127.

Crow, Karen de. Sexist Justice. New York: Vintage, 1975.

Desan, Wilfred. The Marxism of Jean-Paul Sartre. Garden City, N.J.: Doubleday and Co., Inc., 1966.

_____. The Tragic Finale. New York: Harper and Row, 1960.

Dijkstra, Sandra. "Simone de Beauvoir and Betty Friedan the Politics of Omission." Feminist Studies, No. 2, Summer, 1980, pp. 290-303.

Doeuff, Michele Le. "Simone de Beauvoir and Existentialism." Feminist Studies, 6, No. 2, Summer, 1980, pp. 277-289.

Dowling, Collette. The Cinderella Complex. New York: Simon and Schuster, 1981.

Eannes, Elizabeth R. "Sexism and Woman as Object." Journal of Thought, 11, Apr. 1976, pp. 140-143.

Eisenstein, Zillah R. Capitalist Patriarchy and the Case for Socialist Feminism. New York: Monthly Review Press, 1979.

Elliston, Frederick. "In Defense of Promiscuity." In Philosophy and Sex. Eds. Robert Baker and Frederick Elliston. Buffalo: Prometheus, 1975.

Felstiner, Mary Lowenthal. "Seeing the Second Sex Through the Second Wave." Feminist Studies, 6, No. 2, Summer, 1980, pp. 247-276.

Ferguson, Ann. "Androgyny As an Ideal for Human Development," Philosophy and Women (Belmont: Wadsworth, 1979), p. 46.

Foreman, Ann. Feminity as Alienation: Women and the Family in Marxism and Psychoanalysis. London: Pluto Press, 1977.

Freud, Sigmund. Civilization and Its Discontents. Trans. Joan Rivera. Garden City, New York: Doubleday Anchor Books, 1930.

Friedan, Betty. The Feminine Mystique. New York: Dell, 1972.

_____. The Second Stage. New York: Summit Books, 1981.

_____. "Sex, Society and the Female Dilemma: A dialogue Between Simone de Beauvoir and Betty Friedan." Saturday Review, 14, June 1975, pp. 18-20.

Fuchs, Jo-Ann P. "Female Eroticism in the Second Sex." Feminist Studies, 6, No. 2, Summer 1980, pp. 304-313.

Gerrassi, John. "Simone de Beauvoir: The Second Sex 25 Years Later: An interview with Simone de Beauvoir." Society, 13, No. 2, Jan-Feb. 1976.

Gilder, George. Wealth and Poverty. New York: Basic Books, 1981.

Goldberg, Steven. "The Inevitability of Patriarchy." In Sex Equality. Ed. Jane English. Englewood Cliffs, N.J.: Prentice-Hall, 1977, pp. 196-204.

Goldman, Alan. "Plain Sex." Philosophy and Public Affairs, Vol. 6, 3, Spring 1977, pp. 267-287.

Goldman, Emma. "The Tragedy of Woman's Emancipation." In The Feminist Papers. Ed. Alice Rossi. New York: Columbia University Press, 1973, pp. 508-516.

Hanson, Linda. "A Move to Positive Human Relationships: Sartre to de Beauvoir." Diss. Marquette, 1976.

_____. "Pain and Joy in Human Relationships: Jean-Paul Sartre and Simone de Beauvoir." Philosophy Today, 23, Winter, 1979, pp. 338-346.

Hegel, G.W.F. The Phenomenology of Mind. Trans. J.B. Baille. New York: Harper and Row, 1967.

_____. The Philosophy of Hegel. Trans. T.M. Knox. London: Oxford Press, 1967.

Heidegger, Martin. Being and Time. Trans. Macquerrie and
     Robinson. New York: Harper and Row, 1962.

Hill, Sharon Bishop. "Self-Determination and Autonomy."
     Philosophy and Women. Eds. Sharon Bishop and Marjorie
     Weinzweig. Belmont: Wadsworth, 1979, pp. 68-76.

Hume, David. Treatise on Human Nature. London: Oxford Press,
     1973.

Jaggar, Allison. "Political Philosophies of Women's Liberation."
     Philosophy and Women. Eds. Sharon Bishop and Marjorie
     Weinzweig. Belmont: Wadsworth, 1979, 252-257.

Jardine, Alice. "Interview with Simone de Beauvoir." Signs, 5,
     Winter 1979, pp. 224-236.

Jeanson, Francis. Sartre and the Problem of Morality. Trans.
     Robert Stone. Bloomington: Indiana Press, 1980.

John, Helen James. "The Promise of Freedom in the Thought of
     Simone de Beauvoir: How An Infant Smiles." Proc. Cath.
     Phil. Assoc., 50, 1976, pp. 72-81.

Kant, Immanuel. Fundamental Principles of the Metaphysics of
     Morals. Trans. Abbott. Indianapolis: Bobbs-Merrill, 1976.

Kaufmann, Walter, ed. Existentialism from Doestoevsky to Sartre.
     New York: Meridian Books, 1956.

_____. Nietzsche: Philosopher, Psychologist, Antichrist.
     New York; Meridian Books, 1956.

Ketchum, Ann and Pierce, Christine. "Separation and Sexual
     Relationships." Philosophy and Women. Eds. Sharon Bishop
     and Marjorie Weinzweig. Belmont: Wadsworth, 1979, pp. 167-
     171.

King, Thomas W. "Freedom and Nothingness." Proc. New Mexico West
     Texas-Phil. Soc., April 1974, pp. 15-20.

Kojeve, Alexandre. An Introduction to Reading Hegel. Trans.
     James H. Nichols, Jr. New York: Basic Books, 1969.

Labar, Margot de. "Feminism and Morality in the Works of Simone
     de Beauvoir and John Stuart Mill." Masters Thesis, University
     of Kansas, 1977.

Leighton, Jean. Simone de Beauvoir on Women. Rutherford, N.J.:
     Fairleigh Dickinson University Press, 1975.

Markovic, Mihailo. "Women's Liberation and Human Emancipation."
     Philo-Forum, Boston, 5, Fall-Winter 1973, pp. 145-167.

Marx, Karl. The Marx-Engels Reader. Ed. Robert Tucker. New York: Norton, 1972.

McCall, Dorothy Kaufmann. "Simone de Beauvoir, The Second Sex, and Jean-Paul Sartre." Signs, 5, Winter 1979, pp. 209-223.

Mill, John STuart. The Essential Writings of John Stuart Mill. New York: Bantam, 1971._____. "The Subjection of Women." In Essays on Sex Equality . Ed. Alice S. Rosser. Chicago: University of Chicago Press, 1970; also in Women in Western Thought. Ed. Martha Osborne. New York: Random House, 1979.

Mitchell, Juliet. Woman's Estate. New York: Vintage, 1971.

Moulton, Janice. "Sexual Behavior: Another Position." Journal of Philosophy, LXXIII, 16, Sept. 16, 1979, pp. 537-547.

Nietzsche, Friedrich. The Geneaology of Morals. Trans. Walter Kaufmann and R.J. Hollingdale. New York: Vintage, 1969.

_____. The Portable Nietzsche. Trans. Walter Kaufmann. New York: Viking, 1968.

_____. Thus Spoke Zarathustra. Trans. R.J. Hollingdale. New York: Penguin Books, 1969.

O'Driscoll, Lyla H. "On The Nature and Value of Marriage," in Feminism and Philosophy, eds. Vetterling-Braggen, Frederick Elliston, and Jane English. Totowa, New Jersey: Littlefield, Adams and Co., 1977, pp. 249-63.

Osborne, Martha. Women in Western Thought. New York: Random House, 1979.

Plato. The Collected Dialogues. Eds. Hamilton and Cairns. Princeton: Princeton University Press, 1978.

Pompei, Guiliana. "Wages for Housework." Feminist Frameworks, eds. Allison Jagger and Paula Rothenberg-Struhl. New York: McGraw-Hill, 1978.

Popper, Karl. Conjectures and Refutations: The Growth of Scientific Knowledge. New York: Harper and Row, 1965.

Rawls, John. Theory of Justice. Cambridge, Mass.: Belkamp Press, 1971.

Rowbothan, Sheila. Women's Consciousness, Man's World. Baltimore: Penguin, 1973.

Rozak, Theodore. "The Hard and the Soft: The Force of Feminism in Modern Times." In Masculine/Feminine. Eds. Betty and Theodore Rozak. New York: Harper and Row, 1969, pp. 87-104.

Ruether, Rosemary. New Woman/New Earth: Sexist Ideologies and Human Liberation. New York: Seabury, 1978.

St. Paul. Letter to the Romans.

Sartre, Jean-Paul. Anti-Semite and Jew. Trans. G. Becher. New York: Shocken, 1948.

_____. Being and Nothingness. Trans. Hazel Barnes. New York: Washington Square, 1969.

_____. The Critique of Dialectical Reason. Trans. Alan Sheridan-Smith. London: NLB, 1978.

_____. "Existentialism is a Humanism." In Existentialism from Doestoevsky to Sartre. Ed. Walter Kaufmann. New York: Meridian Books, 1956.

_____. Life/Situations: Essays Written and Spoken. Trans. Paul Auster and Lyndin Davis. New York: Pantheon, 1977.

Schwartzer, Alice. "The Radicalization of Simone de Beauvoir." MS., July 1972, pp. 60-62.

_____. "Talking to a Friend - An Interview with Simone de Beauvoir." MS., July 1977, pp. 16-20.

Shapiro, Gary. "Choice and Universality in Sartre's Ethics." Man and World, Vol. 7, No. 1, Feb. 1974, pp. 20-36.

Simons, Margaret Ann. "A Phenomenology of Oppression: A Critical Introduction to 'le Deuxieme Sexe' by Simone de Beauvoir." Diss. Purdue, 1977.

Solomon, Robert. Existentialism. New York: Modern Library, 1974.

_____. "Sexual Paradigms." Journal of Philosophy, LXXXI, No. 11, June 13, 1974, pp. 336-346.

Tormey, Judith. "Exploitation, Oppression, and Self-Sacrifice." Philosophical Forum, 5, 72-74, pp. 206-221.

Trebilcot, Joyce. "Sex Roles: The Argument from Nature." Sex Equality. Ed. James English. Englewood Cliffs, N.J.: Prentice-Hall, 1977.

281

Verne, D.P. ed. Sexual Love and Western Morality: A Philosophical Anthology. New York: Harper and Row, 1972.

Warnock, Mary. Existential Ethics. London: Macmillan, 1967.

Wild, John. "Authentic Existence: A New Approach to 'Value Theory.'" In An Invitation to Phenomenology. Eds. James Die. Chicago: Quadrangle Books Inc., 1965, pp. 59-77.

_____. Existence and the World of Freedom. Englewood Cliffs, N.J.: Prentice-Hall, 1965.

_____. The Challenge of Existentialism. Bloomington: Indiana University Press, 1963.

Zaretsky, Eli. Capitalism: The Family and Personal Life. New York: Harper and Row, 1976.

GLASSBORO STATE COLLEGE